Better Homes and Gardens®

Christmas
1989

TABLE OF CONTENTS

CHRISTMAS IN THE AIR

SYMBOLS
OF THE SEASON

HOME FOR
THE HOLIDAYS

Christmas
In the Air

Remember When

Snowbound Christmas In Colorado

We were waiting for snow that Christmas in Colorado, but nothing fell from a brilliant sky. Joggers were out in shorts, and sunbathers appeared on balconies; my daughter had a sunburn going into Christmas week. From nowhere a few bewildered violets appeared against our front steps. "What next?" I thought. "Perhaps daffodils."

During the night of the twenty-second the blizzard began without warning, and by the next morning Colorado was covered. Soon even the mountains disappeared in the swirl of snow. The first day of the storm, driving became nearly impossible and snowplows abandoned the outskirts of town. I made a flying attempt to get home after work, finally leaving the car in a drift below the steep hill to our house.

Believing we'd awake to find clear skies and the plows at work, my family and I went to bed and slept that deep sleep one falls into during snow or rain. I awoke at first light and went out onto the patio, where the old table I use for a measuring gauge had forty inches piled up, the snow still falling. The wind had stopped, and I could not hear a motor running anywhere. The roads below were without a track. The silence was immense.

It was Christmas Eve morning and I hadn't shopped for Christmas dinner. The fresh turkey I had ordered some time back awaited me at a grocery store 3 miles across town. So did the yams, pearly onions, fresh mincemeat, oysters, and all the other frills that we've always counted as holiday necessities.

I felt the house was like a ship, an unlikely metaphor in a landlocked place, but it would serve: a ship moored in a snow sea with unseen mountainous icebergs.

I started down to the basement, realizing midway that we'd lent our cross-country skis to a friend who expected out-of-state relatives for the week. If we'd had snowshoes, I might have made it to the grocery. I've never owned a pair, despite my Wisconsin-bred father's advice to keep some around for emergencies. They struck me at that moment as rare and valuable possessions, and I promised to get myself a pair as soon as the storm was over.

Surveying the refrigerator, I remembered how clever I'd been to give it one of those grand and sweeping cleanings, making way for holiday foodstuffs. What I found were some scallions, celery, and a head of limp romaine. There were also eggs, two sticks of margarine (imagine—no butter at Christmas!), and some milk. The fruit bowl on the counter held several Granny Smith apples, some oranges, and a pound of pecans in the shells.

Even the pantry was sadly depleted. We'd used up the summer harvest I put by, leaving a few odd jars of jam and pickles.

Under the tree, however, were my mother's annual gifts of Wisconsin wild rice and maple syrup, treasures I usually dole out in stingy amounts through the year. The thought of the Indians out on the lake harvesting rice reminded me of provender I'd forgotten: In my neighbor's freezer down the way were two wild ducks with my name on them. If my neighbor hadn't been clever enough to clean out his freezer, we were in luck (maybe butter!).

I wanted to dance, but instead I lighted a fire and sat down with a cup of coffee to plan the menu. The family was still asleep and the kitchen remained my own, a warm enclosure in a silent world. I felt satisfaction as I jotted down a proper kind of menu, one that might have been prepared for travelers on a luxury liner such as the old *Queen Elizabeth*:

Chopped Duck Livers on Melba Toast
Roasted Wild Duck with Oranges
Wild Rice Dressing
Braised Romaine with Herbed
Scallion Butter
Zucchini Pickles and Tomato Chutney
Apple Salad
Maple Pecan Pie

Later I called our friend whose home we were to visit for champagne and appetizers before dinner. We had planned a two-step Christmas to end at my house with turkey and trimmings. I told her I had everything at hand, except a way to get her and her daughter over here. It turned out they'd bought each other cross-country skis for Christmas, a mutual surprise opened early. They promised to ski over the edge of the foothills and down into our backyard, the wine and stuffed mushrooms in their backpacks.

That afternoon we made a flag, a Christmas pennant to hoist against our fence. We wanted to make sure they'd recognize the place. By Christmas morning the house would surely be buried.

—*Pauline W. Wanderer*

Christmas Is Coming

—Alison Uttley

At Christmas the wind ceased to moan. Snow lay thick on the fields and the woods cast blue shadows across it. The fir trees were like sparkling, gem-laden Christmas trees, the only ones Susan had ever seen. The orchard, with the lacy old boughs outlined with snow, was a grove of fairy trees. The woods were enchanted, exquisite, the trees were holy, and anything harmful had shrunken to a thin wisp and had retreated into the depths.

The fields lay with their unevennesses gone and paths obliterated, smooth white slopes crisscrossed by black lines running up to the woods. More than ever the farm seemed under a spell, like a toy in the forest, with little wooden animals and men; a brown horse led by a stiff little red-scarfed man to a yellow stable door; round, white, woolly sheep clustering round a blue trough of orange mangolds; red cows drinking from a square, white trough, and returning to a painted cow-house.

Footprints were everywhere on the snow, rabbits and foxes, blackbirds, pheasants and partridges, trails of small paws, the mark of a brush, and the long feet of the cock pheasant and the tip-mark of his tail.

A jay flew out of the wood like a blue flashing diamond and came to the grass-plot for bread. A robin entered the house and hopped under the table while Susan sat very still and her father sprinkled crumbs on the floor.

Rats crouched outside the window, peeping out of the walls with gleaming eyes, seizing the birds' crumbs and scraps, and slowly lolloping back again.

continued

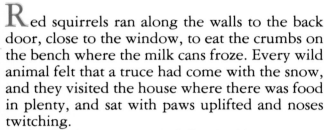

Red squirrels ran along the walls to the back door, close to the window, to eat the crumbs on the bench where the milk cans froze. Every wild animal felt that a truce had come with the snow, and they visited the house where there was food in plenty, and sat with paws uplifted and noses twitching.

For the granaries were full, it had been a prosperous year, and there was food for everyone. Not like the year before when there was so little hay that Mr Garland had to buy a stack in February. Three large haystacks as big as houses stood in the stackyard, thatched evenly and straight by Job Fletcher, who was the best thatcher for many a mile. Great mounds showed where the roots were buried. The brick-lined pit was filled with grains and in the barns were stores of corn.

The old brew-house was full of logs of wood, piled high against the walls, cut from trees which the wind had blown down. The coal-house with its strong ivied walls, part of the old fortress, had been stored with coal brought many a mile in the blaze of summer; twenty tons lay under the snow.

On the kitchen walls hung the sides of bacon and from hooks in the ceiling dangled great hams and shoulders. Bunches of onions were twisted in the pantry and barn, and an empty cow-house was stored with potatoes for immediate use.

The floor of the apple chamber was covered with apples, rosy apples, little yellow ones, like cowslip balls, wizenedy apples with withered, wrinkled cheeks, fat, well-fed smooth-faced apples, and immense green cookers, pointed like a house, which would burst in the oven and pour out a thick cream of the very essence of apples.

Even the cheese chamber had its cheeses this year, for there had been too much milk for the milkman, and the cheese presses had been put into use again. Some of them were Christmas cheese, with layers of sage running through the middles like green ribbons.

Stone jars like those in which the forty thieves hid stood on the pantry floor, filled with white lard, and balls of fat tied up in bladders hung from the hooks. Along the broad shelves round the walls were pots of jam, blackberry and apple, from the woods and orchard, Victoria plum from the trees on house and barn, black currant from the garden, and red currant jelly, damson cheese from the half-wild ancient trees which grew everywhere, leaning over walls, dropping their blue fruit on paths and walls, in pigsty and orchard, in field and water trough, so that Susan thought they were wild as hips and haws.

Pickles and spices filled old brown pots decorated with crosses and flowers, like the pitchers and crocks of Will Shakespeare's time.

In the little dark wine chamber under the stairs were bottles of elderberry wine, purple, thick, and sweet, and golden cowslip wine, and hot ginger, some of them many years old, waiting for the winter festivities.

There were dishes piled with mince pies on the shelves of the larder, and a row of plum puddings with their white calico caps, and strings of sausages, and round pats of butter, with swans and cows and wheat-ears printed upon them.

Everyone who called at the farm had to eat and drink at Christmas-tide.

A few days before Christmas Mr Garland and Dan took a bill-hook and knife and went into the woods to cut branches of scarlet-berried holly. They tied them together with ropes and dragged them down over the fields to the barn. Mr Garland cut a bough of mistletoe from the ancient hollow hawthorn which leaned over the wall by the orchard, and thick clumps of dark-berried ivy from the walls.

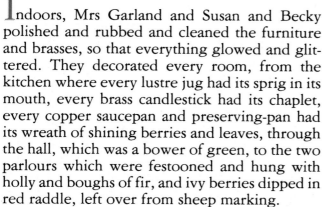

Indoors, Mrs Garland and Susan and Becky polished and rubbed and cleaned the furniture and brasses, so that everything glowed and glittered. They decorated every room, from the kitchen where every lustre jug had its sprig in its mouth, every brass candlestick had its chaplet, every copper saucepan and preserving-pan had its wreath of shining berries and leaves, through the hall, which was a bower of green, to the two parlours which were festooned and hung with holly and boughs of fir, and ivy berries dipped in red raddle, left over from sheep marking.

Holly decked every picture and ornament. Sprays hung over the bacon and twisted round the hams and herb bunches. The clock carried a crown on his head, and every dish-cover had a little sprig. Susan kept an eye on the lonely forgotten humble things, the jelly moulds and colanders and nutmeg-graters, and made them happy with glossy leaves. Everything seemed to speak, to ask for its morsel of greenery, and she tried to leave out nothing.

On Christmas Eve fires blazed in the kitchen and parlour and even in the bedrooms. Becky ran from room to room with the red-hot salamander which she stuck between the bars to make a blaze, and Mrs Garland took the copper warming-pan filled with glowing cinders from the kitchen fire and rubbed it between the sheets of all the beds. Susan had come down to her cosy tiny room with thick curtains at the window, and a fire in the big fireplace. Flames roared up the chimneys as Dan carried in the logs and Becky piled them on the blaze. The wind came back and tried to get in, howling at the key-holes, but all the shutters were cottered and the doors shut. The horses and mares stood in the stables, warm and happy, with nodding heads. The cows slept in the cow-houses, the sheep in the open sheds. Only Rover stood at the door of his kennel, staring up at the sky, howling to the dog in the moon, and then he, too, turned and lay down in his straw.

In the middle of the kitchen ceiling there hung the kissing-bunch, the best and brightest pieces of holly made in the shape of a large ball which dangled from the hook. Silver and gilt drops, crimson bells, blue glass trumpets, bright oranges and red polished apples, peeped and glittered through the glossy leaves. Little flags of all nations, but chiefly Turkish for some unknown reason, stuck out like quills on a hedgehog. The lamp hung near, and every little berry, every leaf, every pretty ball and apple had a tiny yellow flame reflected in its heart.

Twisted candles hung down, yellow, red, and blue, unlighted but gay, and on either side was a string of paper lanterns.

Mrs Garland climbed on a stool and nailed on the wall the Christmas texts, 'God bless our Home', 'God is Love', 'Peace be on this House', 'A Happy Christmas and a Bright New Year'.

So the preparations were made. Susan hung up her stocking at the foot of the bed and fell asleep. But soon singing roused her and she sat, bewildered. Yes, it was the carol-singers.

Outside under the stars she could see the group of men and women, with lanterns throwing beams across the paths and on to the stable door. One man stood apart beating time, another played a fiddle and another had a flute. The rest sang in four parts the Christmas hymns, 'While shepherds watched', 'O come, all ye faithful', and 'Hark the herald angels sing'.

There was the Star, Susan could see it twinkling and bright in the dark boughs with their white frosted layers; and there was the stable. In a few hours it would be Christmas Day, the best day of all the year.

Christmas Crafts For the Home

Dress up your home this holiday season with handsome handcrafted treasures. Here, and on succeeding pages, you'll find a variety of projects you can craft in time for Christmas: a needlepoint wreath, wooden candlesticks and centerpieces, a cross-stitched wall hanging and guest towels, a patchwork table runner, and a greenery wreath and garland.

Holly and Ivy Wreath

Finished stitched wreath design is 20x20 inches.

MATERIALS
31x31-inch piece of 11-count cream Aida cloth
DMC embroidery floss in the following amounts and colors: 2 skeins *each* of light teal (No. 992), dark teal (No. 991), light olive green (No. 470), and gray-green (No. 503); 1 skein *each* of lime green (No. 906), dark olive green (No. 937), pink (No. 893), dark coral (No. 891), peach (No. 352), brown (No. 898), kelly green (No. 911), and off-white (No. 3033)
Graph paper
Colored felt-tip pens

INSTRUCTIONS
The chart on *page 16* represents one-fourth of the design. For best results, using colored pens, chart the complete design onto graph paper before you begin to stitch.

Begin charting at line A-B (9 o'clock) on the design and work to line C-D (12 o'clock). Working *clockwise,* chart the design from A-B to C-D again (3 o'clock). Continue around in this manner two more times to complete the wreath. The shaded portions of the chart below the A-B line show how the shapes interlock as they scroll around the wreath. Do not chart the shaded portion.

Begin stitching the design 6¼ inches from the left edge of the fabric and 15½ inches from the top edge. Work in the same sequence as described for charting. Use two strands of floss to work cross-stitches over one thread of the cloth. When stitching is complete, frame as desired.

Holly wreath

1 Square = 1 Stitch

COLOR KEY

☐ Light teal (992)

☐ Lime green (906)

☐ Peach (352)

■ Dark teal (991)

■ Dark olive green (937)

■ Brown (898)

■ Light olive green (470)

☐ Pink (893)

■ Kelly green (911)

☐ Gray green (503)

■ Dark coral (891)

☐ Off-white (3033)

Christmas Greetings Wall Hanging

COLOR KEY

⊠ Burgundy (044)

◩ Dark Green (0246)

◉ Gold (0309)

▣ Gray (0401)

⊡ Light Green (0243)

◎ Red (047)

⊡ Yellow (0307)

Poinsettia Guest Towels

Poinsettia design is 110 stitches wide and 26 stitches high.

MATERIALS
(for 2 towels)
2 terry cloth hand towels with even-weave fabric bands
DMC embroidery floss: 1 skein *each* of bright Christmas red (666), light Christmas green (701), and topaz (725)
Embroidery hoop
Tapestry needle

INSTRUCTIONS
Referring to the pattern *below,* chart the design on graph paper. Mark the center. Baste center of even-weave band on each towel.

Use three plies of floss and work the cross-stitches over one thread of even-weave.

Stitch yellow French knots at dots on poinsettia design. Add checks or stripes along border.

Christmas-Greetings Wall Hanging

Finished size is 8⅛x10 inches. Design is 75 stitches wide and 91 stitches high.

MATERIALS
16x18-inch piece of white 18-count Aida cloth
Susan Bates Anchor embroidery floss: 1 skein *each* of burgundy (44), dark green (246), gold (309), gray (401), light green (243), red (47), and yellow (307)
Embroidery hoop
Tapestry needle

INSTRUCTIONS
Referring to pattern on page 17, chart design onto graph paper.

Use three plies of floss and work cross-stitches over two threads of Aida cloth. Measure 4 inches down from top and 4 inch-es in from left side; begin stitching upper-left corner of border here. Frame wall hanging as desired.

Greeting Card

Finished size of stitchery is 4⅜x2¼ inches.
Design is 63x33 stitches.

MATERIALS
4x6-inch piece of perforated paper
Small amounts of embroidery floss in same colors as Christmas-Greetings Wall Hanging
Blank greeting card
Spray adhesive; tapestry needle

INSTRUCTIONS
Use three plies of floss.

Measure ¾ inch down from top and ¾ inch in from left side of paper; begin stitching upper-left corner of border here. Work burgundy border to 63 stitches wide and 33 stitches high. Referring to pattern for Christmas-Greetings Wall Hanging on page 17, stitch greetings and candle motif from upper portion of chart, inside border. Trim paper ⅜ inch past border. Affix stitchery to card with adhesive.

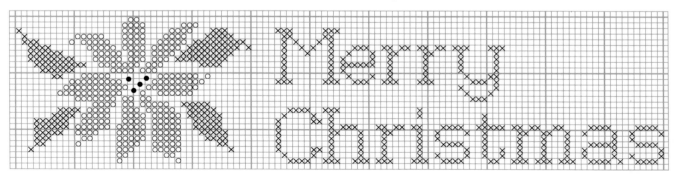

COLOR KEYS

▢ **Bright Christmas Red (666)**   ⊠ **Light Christmas Green (701)**

Guest Towels

One of the traditional symbols of Christmas, the star, inspired this handsome trio of trims. Beautifully designed and crafted, these wooden decorations are sure to add sparkle to a holiday table or brighten a corner—and they work up in a twinkling.

Star Tree Centerpiece

Tree stands 12 inches high.

MATERIALS
5-foot length of 1x10-inch fir
10-inch length of ⅜-inch-
  diameter dowel
Paint primer
Red, green, and yellow acrylic
  paints
Satin varnish
Carpenter's glue

INSTRUCTIONS
Trace the small star pattern on page 23 onto tracing paper. Next, enlarge the pattern in ⅛-inch increments to make six more star patterns. Then, decrease the star pattern in ⅛-inch increments to make four more patterns. Trace the patterns onto wood.

From fir, cut out two stars from the smallest pattern and one from each of the remaining star patterns. Cut one 4-inch-diameter circle for the tree base.

With a ⅜-inch drill bit, drill holes through center of 11 stars (do not drill a hole through the center of one of the smallest stars) and through the center of the tree base. Drill a 1-inch-deep hole between legs of two star points of remaining small star for treetop. Sand and prime all pieces (tops, bottoms, and sides).

Glue dowel into center of base; check to be sure it is perpendicular to the base. Allow this assembly to dry completely.

With red, paint base of tree; with yellow, paint star treetop; with green, paint remaining stars and dowel. When dry, coat all pieces with varnish.

Stack 11 green stars onto dowel in order of size, from largest to smallest; top with yellow star.

Star Candlesticks

Shown on page 22.

Candlesticks stand 3 inches high.

MATERIALS
2 feet of 1x10-inch fir for
  2 candlesticks
2 wood candle cups
Wood primer
Red and green acrylic paints
Carpenter's glue
Polyurethane satin varnish
Antique glazing
Two 1-inch No. 7 wood
  screws

INSTRUCTIONS
Trace star patterns on page 23 onto tracing paper. For two candlesticks, trace two large stars and two small stars onto wood. Cut out shapes. Sand and prime all pieces. Paint tops and sides of the large stars green; paint tops and sides of small stars and candle cups red. When dry, coat with varnish.

Center and glue small star atop large star. Center and glue candle cup atop small star. For added strength, set screw through candle cup base. (The cups come with a countersink and shank hole in the bottom for a No. 7 screw.) To complete, apply antique glazing with a soft cloth, following the manufacturer's instructions.

Star Centerpiece

Finished size of centerpiece is 13x13 inches; it stands approximately 4 inches tall.

MATERIALS
5-foot length of 1x6-inch fir
4 candle cups
Wood primer
Red and green acrylic paints
Carpenter's glue
Satin varnish
Antique glazing
Eight 5d finishing nails
Four 4d finishing nails
Eight 1½-inch No. 7 screws

INSTRUCTIONS

STARS: From fir, cut nine stars using the small star pattern on page 23. Set eight stars aside. From the remaining star, cut four standing posts (supports) for the four stars that sit in center of sides, using the dashed lines on small star pattern. Discard remains of star. Sand and prime all pieces and the four candle cups. Paint the stars red; paint the candle cups and standing posts green.

BASE: Cut ¾-inch-square strips from scrap piece of ¾-inch fir. Miter the strips to 9 inches for outside length. Join the strips to form a frame. Use glue and 4d finishing nails. Once you have joined all sides, check to be sure frame is square. Let frame sit until the glue is dry. Apply primer; let dry. Paint the frame green.

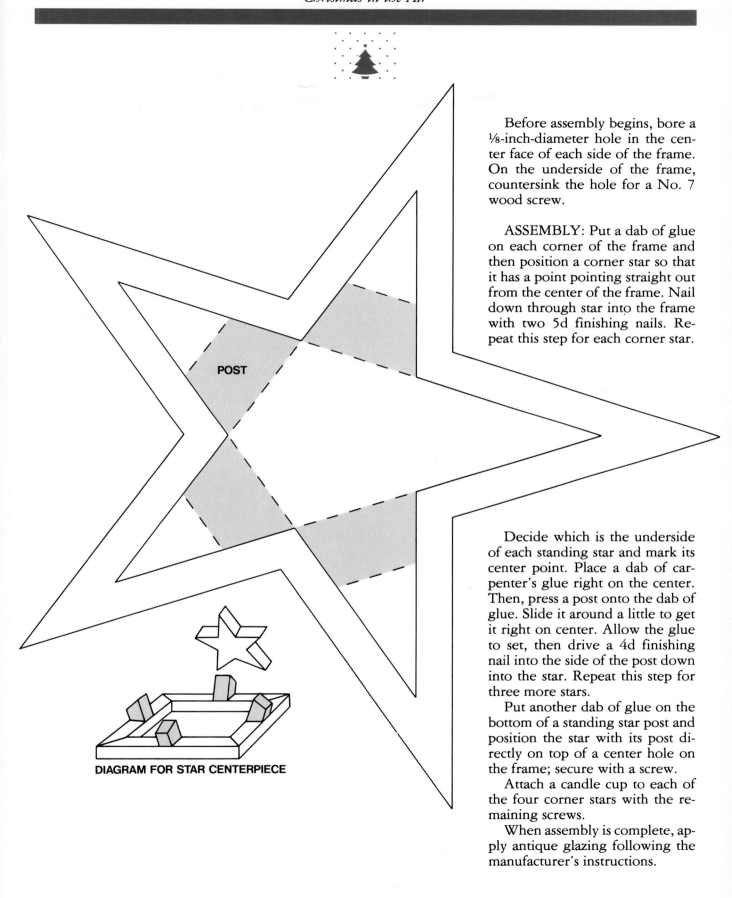

POST

DIAGRAM FOR STAR CENTERPIECE

Before assembly begins, bore a ⅛-inch-diameter hole in the center face of each side of the frame. On the underside of the frame, countersink the hole for a No. 7 wood screw.

ASSEMBLY: Put a dab of glue on each corner of the frame and then position a corner star so that it has a point pointing straight out from the center of the frame. Nail down through star into the frame with two 5d finishing nails. Repeat this step for each corner star.

Decide which is the underside of each standing star and mark its center point. Place a dab of carpenter's glue right on the center. Then, press a post onto the dab of glue. Slide it around a little to get it right on center. Allow the glue to set, then drive a 4d finishing nail into the side of the post down into the star. Repeat this step for three more stars.

Put another dab of glue on the bottom of a standing star post and position the star with its post directly on top of a center hole on the frame; secure with a screw.

Attach a candle cup to each of the four corner stars with the remaining screws.

When assembly is complete, apply antique glazing following the manufacturer's instructions.

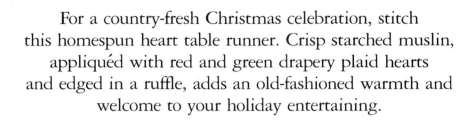

For a country-fresh Christmas celebration, stitch
this homespun heart table runner. Crisp starched muslin,
appliquéd with red and green drapery plaid hearts
and edged in a ruffle, adds an old-fashioned warmth and
welcome to your holiday entertaining.

Heart Table Runner

Runner is 16x64 inches, including ruffle.

MATERIALS
2 yards of 45-inch-wide muslin
12x60-inch piece of fleece
½ yard of 54-inch-wide red plaid fabric for ruffle
Scraps of red-and-green plaid fabrics for 24 hearts
4¼ yards of cotton cording
Strip of plaid fabric pieced to measure 1½ inches wide and 4¼ yards long for piping
Water-erasable pen

INSTRUCTIONS
Note: ½-inch seam allowances are used throughout unless noted otherwise.

Cut two pieces of muslin to measure 13x61 inches. Set one of the pieces aside for backing. Using a water-erasable pen, at *each* end of one muslin piece and inside the seam allowance, draw a 9x12-inch rectangle. Divide the rectangle into 3-inch squares (there will be three rows, with four squares in each row).

Center and baste the fleece to the unmarked side of the muslin. Machine-quilt atop the drawn lines.

Trace heart pattern *below* onto tissue paper; cut out. Trace 24 hearts onto *wrong* side of assorted plaids; do not cut out. With right sides facing, place muslin scraps behind the heart drawings and stitch around the entire heart shapes. Cut out the hearts, leaving ¼-inch seams; clip curves. Make a small slit in the centers of the muslin; turn the hearts right side out and press.

Hand-appliqué the hearts atop each of the 24 squares.

For the piping, cover the cotton cording with 1½-inch-wide plaid fabric. Stitch piping atop seam line of right side of muslin.

For the ruffle, cut six 3-inch-wide strips the full width of the plaid fabric. Piece strips to measure 9 yards long; sew strip together to form a circle.

Press under ¼ inch twice along one long edge; machine-stitch for narrow hem.

Stitch two rows of gathering threads along opposite edge of ruffle. Pull up gathers to fit edges of runner. With right sides facing, sew ruffle atop piping seam line.

With right sides facing, sew the backing to the runner top, keeping ruffle free from seam and leaving a 6-inch opening for turning. Clip seams, turn, and press. Sew opening closed.

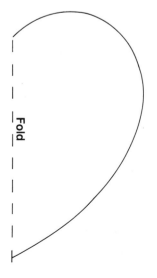

Fold

Greenery Wreath And Garland

MATERIALS

Cut greenery
Wire ring or straw wreath ring
Pruning clippers
Wire cutters
No. 24 or No. 28 wire
Baler twine or nylon twine

INSTRUCTIONS

GREENS: Gather unwanted branches from evergreen shrubs, if possible. Juniper, arborvitae, spruce, yew, cedar, and white pine are good candidates. Avoid hemlock; it dries out and drops needles rapidly.

Or, combine various types of evergreens. Lemon leaves and other types of greens available in your area also may be used.

The amount of greens you will need will depend on the size of the handfuls you use and the size of your wreath or the length of your garland.

To prevent moisture loss, clip greens from your yard as soon as possible and store them in a plastic bag in a cool place until you assemble the wreaths and garlands. If you wait until mid-December to gather greens, the winter weather may have dried them out and turned them brownish, and the branches may drop needles as you handle them.

WREATH ASSEMBLY: Cut evergreen boughs to identical lengths; 6 to 7 inches is a convenient length. Lay a handful of greens on a wire ring or straw wreath ring and use No. 24 or No. 28 wire to tightly wrap the greens to the ring. (You must pull the wire tight, so use the lighter wire, No. 28, if you don't have much strength in your hands.)

Attach additional handfuls of greenery, using each to cover the cut ends of the previous attachment, as illustrated *below, left.* Keep all of the handfuls the same size.

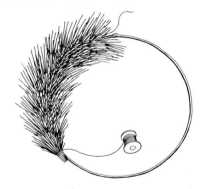

When you complete the ring, lift the top of the first handful and stuff the cut ends of the last handful underneath before wrapping.

Decorate the wreath by wiring on a large bow, pinecones, small bows, candy canes, fruit, nuts, holly, or Christmas tree ornaments.

GARLAND ASSEMBLY: Use the same technique to assemble garlands. Instead of using a wire or straw ring, however, tie handfuls of evergreens to a length of dark-colored baler twine or nylon twine. Fasten one end of the twine to something secure so you can pull the cord taut as you wire the greens in place.

Mist your wreaths or garlands occasionally to keep them from drying out too quickly.

Plain and Paper-Punch Luminarias

MATERIALS

Brown paper lunch bags*
Sand
Plumber's candles or votives
Paper punch; pencil

INSTRUCTIONS

PLAIN: Fill the bottoms of brown paper bags with sand to a depth of 2 inches. Place a candle in each bag of sand, making sure the candles do not touch the sides of the bags.

PAPER-PUNCH: Close up the brown paper bags. Draw three evenly spaced curved lines along both edges of the paper bags. Punch holes along the lines, folding the bags as needed to allow the punch to reach the ends of the lines.

Fill the paper bags with sand to a depth of 2 inches. Place a candle in each bag of sand, making sure the candles do not touch the sides of the bags.

Note: If you prefer, you can purchase special luminaria paper bags that come in assorted colors and with cutouts in traditional holiday shapes.

DISPLAY: Set the paper bags along the edges of walkways, driveways, and patios. For safety, do not leave lighted candles unattended.

For Christmas

Now not a window small or big
But wears a wreath of holly sprig;
Nor any shop too poor to show
Its spray of pine or mistletoe.
Now city airs are spicy-sweet
With Christmas trees along each street,
Green spruce and fir whose boughs will hold
Their tinsel balls and fruits of gold.
Now postman pass in threes and fours
Like bent, blue-coated Santa Claus.
Now people hurry to and fro
With little girls and boys in tow,
And not a child but keeps some trace
Of Christmas secrets in his face.

—*Rachel Field*

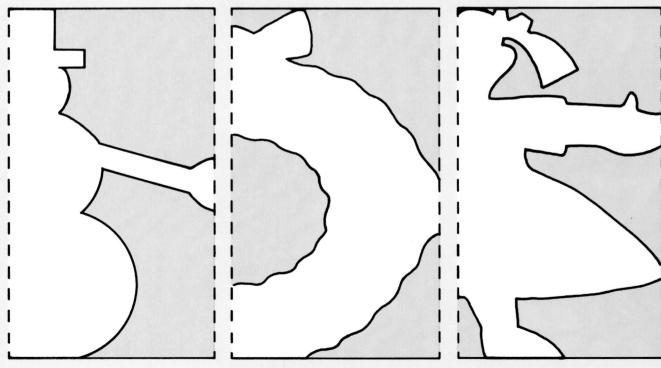

Cards and Trims

Using only paint, paper, and toothbrushes, your kids can create their own Christmas cards. A pair of scissors and some paper are all they'll need for paper chains to tape around packages or loop around the tree.

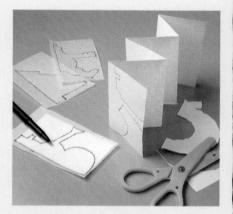

Christmas Chains

MATERIALS
Lightweight white paper
 (watercolor, kraft, or
 construction paper)
Tracing paper
Pen or pencil
Scissors

INSTRUCTIONS
Use tracing paper and a pen or pencil to copy the patterns, *below* and *opposite*. Cut white paper into long strips that are 4 inches deep. To cut the paper, fold the first piece of the paper strip so that it is 2½ inches wide. Continue folding the strip accordion- or fan-style. See photograph, *right*.

Lay the pattern on top of the folded paper strip and trace the shape onto the top section of paper. Cut out the shape through all layers of paper. Open the folded paper to see the chain.

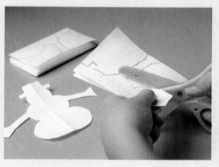

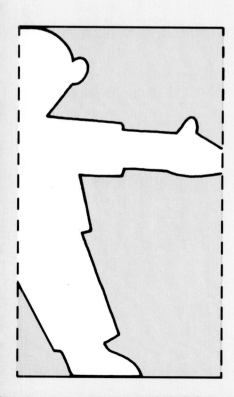

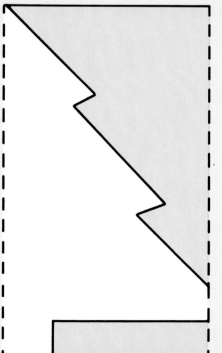

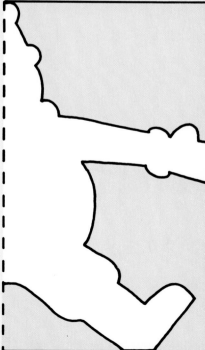

Splatter Cards

MATERIALS
Construction paper
Acrylic paints
Tracing paper

Old toothbrushes (one for
each color paint)
Pen or pencil
Scissors
Newspaper or brown kraft
paper

INSTRUCTIONS
Trace the patterns, *opposite,* onto paper. Cut out the shapes. Fold one 8½x11-inch piece of construction paper in half widthwise for each card. Lay the card on kraft paper or newspaper.

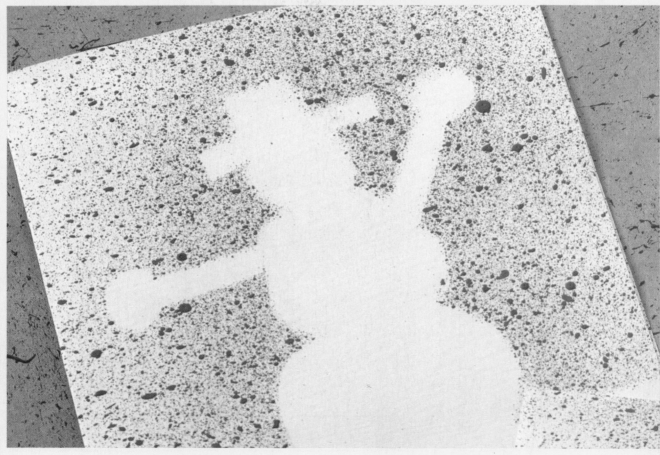

Lay one of the patterns on top of the card. Dip a toothbrush into the paint. Tap the brush on the edge of the paint jar to get rid of the extra paint. Then, hold the brush over the card with one hand, and run the index finger of your other hand through the bristles. Splatter all of the area not covered by the pattern.

Let the paint dry before you try to pick a pattern piece off the card.

Ballyutility's Christmas Tree

—Janet McNeill

Maybe you know the village of Ballyutility. If you've been through it in the train you must have noticed the tidy back gardens, all planted out with orderly potatoes and plump cabbages—there isn't a square inch of ground wasted or a pod of peas that could hold another pea. If you go through the single street you'll find there isn't much in the way of front gardens—most of the houses just have a little square of gravel, except the house at the corner where there is a straggling fir tree. You won't find any children playing in the street either—they've generally got something better to do, and nobody whistles, except to call up a dog. Nobody sings either, except the children in the school, and that's a lesson, so it's different. And when a stranger goes by the dogs take it in turns to bark. That's what it's like in Ballyutility.

Or rather that's what it was like. But something happened last Christmas in Ballyutility, and that's what I want to tell you about. Early in December if you'd gone through the village you'd hardly have known what month it was. You might have heard the children in the school practising carols for the Boxing Day Concert in aid of the Deserving Poor, but there wasn't any sign of Christmas to be seen in any of the three shop windows—the Grocer, the Chemist or the Post Office. Everyone was busy in Ballyutility, but then everybody always was. Mr Jamison, the Grocer, was perhaps the busiest of all—he certainly thought he was. But he didn't festoon his shop with paper chains just because Christmas was coming, nor did he spread it over with artificial frost, or put blobs of cottonwool hanging on strings down the window to look like snow. It wasn't that he didn't know all about these things, for when he was a boy Mr Jamison was apprenticed to his uncle who had a grocer's shop in Belfast, and the week before Christmas his uncle and he had stayed late night after night, sticking blobs of cottonwool on bits of string, till the

window was a whirling fairyland, and neither of them grudged the time they spent at it or the clearing up afterwards. But since he had set up shop for himself in Ballyutility Mr Jamison had changed. 'A shop's a shop, not a scene out of a pantomime,' he said. So though the window was full of raisins and sultanas and currants, of candied peel and almonds, of cherries and preserved ginger, of nutmeg and cinnamon and spice and icing sugar, they all sat in their packets in neat and tidy rows, and there wasn't a cottonwool snowflake or a sprig of holly to be seen.

While Mr Jamison was busy making money in his shining shop Mrs Jamison was busy in her shining house, bringing up Anna and Effie and Jane and little Ben. Effie and Jane and little Ben had just got over the whooping cough, and what with wrapping them up in extra warm mufflers every time they went out and unwrapping them again every time they came in, she had been busier than usual. Perhaps that was why she didn't notice how much of her time Anna was spending in the house next door. Mrs McIlvenny and Hughie lived in the house next door—it was the corner house, the one with the fir tree outside it—and Anna and Hughie were the same age, and had always been great friends. But Hughie had spent a year in a hospital in Belfast and was just home and had a couple of months yet to lie in bed.

A couple of days before Christmas Mrs Jamison went into her back garden to hang out her dishcloths and found Mrs McIlvenny doing the same thing in hers. 'How's Hughie keeping today?' asked Mrs Jamison, taking the last of the clothes-pegs out of her mouth.

'He's coming on,' said Mrs McIlvenny, 'but it's not a thing you can hurry. Your Anna is up in the room with him now.'

'Is that where Anna is?' said Mrs Jamison, rather vexed. 'She slipped off when she had the dishes done, and I don't believe she has her

lessons half learned. Will you call her down for me?'

'Ah, don't call her down,' Mrs McIlvenny begged, 'Hughie's always extra glad to see Anna. She helps him to put in his time.'

'It seems a sin to have that much time to waste,' Mrs Jamison said, and suddenly wondered what she was thinking of, wasting her own time gossiping over the garden fence. There was plenty to do in the house without this. So she hurried indoors and took out her knitting, and was soon busy on the pair of gloves she was making for little Ben's Christmas present. The pattern book she was using said white fluffy wool with scarlet rabbits embroidered on them,

but Mrs Jamison was doing them in grey, which was much more serviceable, and leaving out the rabbits. Even little Ben had enough sense to know that rabbits weren't scarlet! So she sat and knitted, making the needles click and dance up and down the rows, and listened to Effie and Jane murmuring and whooping over their homework, and she wished Anna would come home instead of wasting her time next door with Hughie McIlvenny.

But Anna wasn't wasting her time; she was sitting on the end of Hughie's bed, with her schoolbag on her knee, and the two of them were very busy indeed.

continued

35

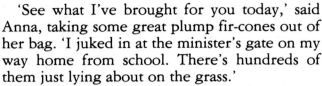

'See what I've brought for you today,' said Anna, taking some great plump fir-cones out of her bag. 'I juked in at the minister's gate on my way home from school. There's hundreds of them just lying about on the grass.'

'Those are grand,' said Hughie, 'but there's only a wee lick of the silver paint left at the bottom of the bottle. What else have you got, Anna?'

She dived into the bag again. 'Here's the tops off the lemonade bottles from the shop. If we hang them in long strings they'll turn in the wind, and the lights will shine on them.'

'They'll be like strings of stars,' Hughie cried. 'What else have you?'

'Silver paper from tangerines, and gold paper off the vinegar bottles,' Anna said, smoothing the shining sheets lovingly, 'but wait till you see here! Easy, Hughie, you'll have them broken.'

'What is it?' Hughie breathed, his eyes alight.

'The electric fused at the Bible Class on Wednesday, and when Mr Simpson was changing the bulbs I got him to give me the duds. You could paint them up with shiny paint, couldn't you, Hughie?'

'They had real lights that lit up on the Christmas tree at the Hospital,' said Hughie, 'green lights and blue lights and red lights. I wish we had real lights.'

'It's no good wishing,' Anna said stoutly, 'but if I fix my bicycle lamp at the bottom of the tree it'll throw its light up through the branches. And there'll be the light from the street lamp, and the light from your room.'

'Did you bring *Her?*' Hughie asked.

'I did. Here she is,' said Anna, tenderly unwrapping the tissue paper from her last package, 'look Hughie!'

Hughie gasped. 'My—oh! Isn't she grand? Why do you never play with her, Anna?'

'Mother says dolls are a waste of time,' Anna answered; 'it was my Auntie from Belfast that bought her for me—the same Auntie that gave me the yellow beads. I never got wearing them either. Mother put them away.'

'She's a beauty,' said Hughie, taking the doll carefully in his hands, 'I'll make her wings and a little wand, and a silver crown for her hair.'

'Oh, Hughie,' cried Anna, in sudden distress, 'I've just thought! What'll we do if it rains? Look at her lovely curly hair! She'll be ruined!'

'It'll not rain,' Hughie said, lying back again on his pillows, for he was tired with the excitement, 'it couldn't rain on Christmas Eve.'

Hughie was right, it didn't rain. Christmas Eve was fine and still and starlit. But the shops shut at their usual time in Ballyutility, for everyone had made shopping lists, and had bought their presents long ago. There were no carol singers about either, because the school children were to sing their carols at the Boxing Day Concert (in aid of the Fund for the Deserving Poor) so there wasn't any need for them to sing them twice, was there? Ballyutility village street was deserted, everyone was indoors having their tea or tying up their presents with brown paper and string—brown paper that would come in useful for parcels afterwards—so no one saw Anna Jamison when she came cautiously out of her back-door, carrying her mother's step-ladder.

Half an hour later the schoolmistress, who had not lived long enough in Ballyutility to be as clever at arranging her Christmas as everyone else, stepped out into the street to post a Christmas card to an aunt whom she had forgotten about. But no sooner had she stepped out than she stepped back again, and called to Tommy, her landlady's little boy, who was cleaning the shoes in the scullery to 'come and look'.

'I declare to goodness,' said Tommy wonderingly, as he stood in the doorway with the blacking brushes still in his hands, 'I declare to goodness—it's—a Christmas Tree.'

'Come on in out of that, Tommy,' his mother called, 'what are you standing there for? There's a whole pile of shoes waiting on you.'

'This is one night they may wait,' declared Tommy, and banging down the brushes he was away out into the street, hatless and coatless, knocking on Mrs Jamison's door.

'Come on,' he cried, hammering on the door with his fists, 'come on till you see! Effie! Jane! Come on out, the whole lot of you. The tree! The tree!' *continued*

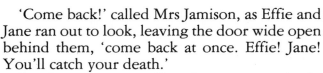

'Come back!' called Mrs Jamison, as Effie and Jane ran out to look, leaving the door wide open behind them, 'come back at once. Effie! Jane! You'll catch your death.'

But it was no use telling them to come back. For they were away—to stand—and gaze—and run and knock on other doors, and bring more wondering children to see the fir tree, transformed in all its fantastic finery, jewelled and adorned, and magically lit by the bicycle lamp, the street lamp, and the light that poured down from Hughie's bedroom. And Hughie from his window was looking down on a flower-bed of children's faces, upturned to the tree, fringed by a crowd of anxious mothers who had followed them out with coats and scarves.

'All those strings of shining stars,' declared one child, as the wind set the lemonade tops swinging and turning, 'as many stars as there are in the sky.'

'What a lot of time it must have taken,' said his mother who was standing behind him, 'and what a waste of time too!'

'What a waste!' echoed the children dutifully.

'Silver fir cones,' cried a little girl, 'just as if they were all covered with frost. Look how beautifully they sparkle!'

'What a waste of paint!' declared her mother, and the children breathed again in chorus. 'What a waste! What a waste!'

'Would you look at the fairy at the top!' piped up the smallest girl of all, 'golden wings she has! And a crown! And look at her lovely hair!'

'If it rains,' said her mother, 'her hair will be ruined. What a waste! It will all be wasted!'

'What a waste!' cried the children all together, 'what a lovely waste! What a lovely, *lovely* waste!'

Then they were all very quiet. Someone in the back row called out, 'Here's Mr Jamison coming!' and everybody stood back a little to let Mr Jamison through.

'A crowd in the streets at this time of night!' he declared. 'These children ought to be in their beds. What's it all about? What sort of a carry-on's this? A tree! A Christmas tree!'

'Isn't it lovely, Mr Jamison?' said the smallest girl of all, without taking her eyes off the tree. 'Look at those stars—and the fairy at the top.'

Mr Jamison stood and looked. Then he said slowly, 'It needs the snow. That's what it needs—the snow.'

One boy at the back, who was bolder than the others, piped up:

Good King Wenceslas looked out
On the Feast of Stephen,
When the snow lay round about
Deep and crisp and even.

And before he had finished the verse they were all singing with him.

So Ballyutility had its Christmas Eve—and its Christmas, too. Little Ben Jamison, who had slept through all the excitement, was taken out by his big sister Anna on Christmas morning. Anna was wearing her yellow beads, and first he pulled at these, but when he saw the tree he crowed and chuckled and clapped his hands which were fine and warm in the new gloves his mother had given him (with scarlet rabbits on the backs—his mother had sat up very late when she went in from the Christmas tree the night before). Although there were now no lights on the tree it looked just as lovely, for it was covered with cascades of cottonwool snow from head to foot. (Mr Jamison had knocked up the chemist and bought all the cottonwool in the shop, and he had gone to bed very late too.)

If you try to visit Ballyutility now you won't be able to find it because they've changed the name of the place. The new name was in the paper the other day; they'd won a prize for the best display of flowers in the village street. The new name is much nicer than the old one was. They chose it just because they liked the sound of it. It's a beautiful name, but it doesn't mean a thing.

—*from A Pinch of Salt*

The Dear Old Tree

BY LUELLA WILSON SMITH

There's a dear old tree, an evergreen tree,
And it blossoms once a year.
'Tis loaded with fruit from top to root,
And it brings to all good cheer.

For it's blossoms bright are small candles white
And it's fruit is dolls and toys.
And they all are free for both you and me
If we're good little girls & boys.

CHRISTMAS GAZETTE

Keeping Christmas:
DECORATIONS

Dress up your house this holiday season with some extra-special decorative touches: flowering plants, heavenly fragrances, festive trims, fanciful table settings, and more. Looking for specifics? On the next four pages you'll find dozens of ways to spread the warmth and beauty of Christmas to every corner of your house.

Mantels
Though you'll never go wrong with evergreen boughs and red candles, why not try something new on the mantel this year.

Decorate your mantel in white. Drape with lace runners, then load the mantelpiece with white candles in glass dishes and candlesticks. Add old-time paper cards, cut-outs, and ornaments.

Show off those collectibles you love: spatterware, small toys, bottles, pewter, cups and saucers—whatever you collect. For the best effect, stick to one collection.

Place a miniature evergreen tree or bush in a terra-cotta planter on each side of the mantelpiece, decorate the trees with tiny potpourri wreaths, and add a shallow terra-

cotta bowl of potpourri in the center.

Wooden bobbins are available in a variety of sizes. Select a medium-size bobbin, tie a ribbon around the shaft, and pair it with a glass hurricane chimney for an eye-catching candle holder atop the mantel.

Centerpieces
Add a festive center-piece to a kitchen, dining room, or hallway table and

watch your home blossom into instant holiday showiness.

Re-create a customary holiday decoration that's as popular today as it was in colonial times. Arrange fresh fruit on a purchased spiked wooden form, then tuck in the leaves and sprigs of greens to make a traditional Williamsburg tabletop tree. Its welcoming scent will fill the whole room for the holidays!

Treat your tabletop to a do-it-yourself candy-cane vase. Glue candy canes to a plastic container, seal them with varnish, and tie on a bow.

Fill your fanciest cut-crystal bowl with fruits, then line the bowl with lemon leaves purchased from a florist.

Use cored red apples as holders for thick white plumber's candles. Group them on a tray or footed cake stand.

Borrow an idea from Easter—dye eggs red

and green and place them on a bed of excelsior.

Create a glitzy display of golden jingle bells in a crystal bowl. Then, add a snippet of greenery and a bright red ribbon for some traditional cheer.

Arrange Bosc pears in a pasta bowl with a garland of silver beads. Set it off with a pine-bough place mat.

Cradle a special present in a spectacular art glass bowl or place

some of your Christmas tree ornaments in a crystal bowl.

Give a mixing bowl a new personality with a candle, pine branches, fresh flowers, and beads.

Set small pillar candles in a bowl of coarse snowy-white salt. Fill the bowl to the brim with salt, then set in as many candles as you like. Any drips will be caught by the salt.

An assortment of candles is a perfect centerpiece for Christmas Eve dinner or midnight supper. For holders, cut hearts of various sizes from pine and attach them to a base. Insert candles in balls of twine or string, or make a hole in the top of an apple or orange.

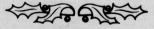

Trees and flowers

Deck out your tree in one of these terrific trims: ornaments that hold favorite family photos; hand-blown glass balls paired with pearls and lace; or dinosaur, alphabet, and Santa ornaments.

Consider these popular varieties when shopping for a fresh Christmas tree. Scotch pine, the top seller, is long-needled and has a true green color. Douglas fir, number-two selling tree, is short-needled, with a blue-gray hue. White pine has soft branches and needles that lend themselves to garlands. Balsam fir retains its needles well. The new Virginia pine is a variety developed especially for the warmer southern climate.

To make ornaments for decorating your Christmas tree, stir up a batch of your favorite cutout cookies, then bake and decorate

them in festive shapes and colors. Use a straw to poke a hole in the tops of cutout cookies before baking. Then hang them on your Christmas tree.

Poinsettias come in a variety of hues: red, pink, white, marbled, and even speckled versions. You can take your choice of shapes and sizes as well. There are tiny, 6-inch plants, along with poinsettia trees now available in

three sizes: the bonsai (18 to 22 inches tall), the mini (28 to 34 inches tall), and the standard (48 to 54 inches tall).

For more variety, try the low-growing poinsettia, which is suitable for hanging baskets as well as centerpieces.

The leaves, flowers, and berries of many plants are toxic; never use them on or near food: amaryllis, poinsettia, mistletoe, bittersweet, yew, balsam fir, crown-of-thorns, and holly.

Decorate the family tree with collections. Place a grouping of antique teddy bears or other stuffed animals beneath the tree in and around wrapped packages. Tie old toy cars to the tree's branches with plaid ribbons. Other collections that can double as tree ornaments are small dolls, cookie cutters, old postcards or greeting cards, and small baskets.

Festive Accents
You don't need a mantel, or traditional red or green, for

Christmas stockings. Try a door or bedpost.

Bring out the old to ring in the new. Put personal collections on display. Nestle old-time toys from your attic in a wagon to add a warm touch to one of your holiday rooms.

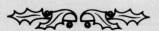

Table Settings
Try one of these dazzling table-dressing ideas for your next holiday get-together.

Go for the gold. Start with white dishes and linens, then add gold doilies, leaves, and tiny bags— as well

as gold ribbon and candles. Put a gold mesh tree ornament at each guest's place.

Make a bouquet of greens and ivy for each place setting. Use glass liners (service plates or chargers) to hold the bouquets; skip the tablecloth to keep the setting woodsy.

By each guest's plate set a mason jar filled with cookies (for dessert or a gift) and stenciled with the guest's name.

Snap a photo of guests as each arrives at your door, put the pictures into tiny frames, and use them as place cards.

Wired together as a wreath, jingle bells shape an elegant napkin ring that doubles as an ornament.

A fresh green wreath with a napkin bow at each place mat makes the simplest dessert a special event. Clip branches and wire them to a wreath form large enough to encircle your plates.

Gift-wrap cardboard squares or rectangles and tie with ribbon to create a Christmas present place mat.

Tuck silverware into mittens and use a scarf as a table runner.

Have the kids make a holiday tablecloth and napkins using heat-set fabric crayons. Add a new drawing each year for happy Christmas memories.

Using a permanent marker, identify each guest's place with a personalized Christmas ornament cradled in a wineglass.

Tie candy canes and silverware with a Christmas bow as a spritely surprise greeting and tasty treat for after the meal.

A quilt-batting snowman on a saucer sled will add a cheerful wintry touch to each place setting at a holiday

table. Craft Frosty from three plastic-foam balls wrapped in quilt batting. Then add facial features: button eyes, a bead mouth, and a tiny carrot nose.

Pine boughs clipped from the base of a Christmas tree create a natural foil for simple tableware. Add clusters of pinecones at each place to reinforce the rustic look.

Scatter Christmas tree tinsel and silver stars cut from cardboard all over the table for a glittery feast. An icy blue tablecloth and antique silver add to the gala effect.

Stitch small bells to the ends of Christmas-plaid ribbons, then tie the ribbons into big bows around the stem of glasses.

Fragrances

Part of the charm of Christmas is its delightful smells—from the

fragrant scent of evergreens to the delicious aroma of freshly baked cookies.

Fill a small saucepan with water; add cloves, orange sections, and cinnamon to the water. Let the mixture simmer on the stove to release a spicy scent.

Make pomander balls by sticking whole cloves in lemons, apples, or oranges, then gently rolling the fruit in a mixture of ground cinnamon, cloves, nutmeg, allspice, and powdered orris root. Suspend the balls in a warm, dry place, such as a closet,

for one week. Then, hang the pomanders throughout the house.

For extra-special holiday scents, fill a pretty bowl with fragrant potpourri or hang tiny bags of the potpourri on your Christmas tree.

Wreaths

Tired of decking your halls with traditional boughs of holly and evergreen but short on ideas? Try one of the fanciful alternatives.

Cover a plastic foam wreath with ribbon bows and tiny stuffed animals, toy soldiers, or other small ornaments.

Tie jewel-toned or paisley ribbons through the twists of a willow wreath, or embellish an

evergreen wreath with pastel silk flowers and ribbons.

Hang pepper or chili wreaths, or those made of dried corn husks.

Individualize a lush evergreen wreath with kitchen gadgets tied with ribbons.

Nestle a bouquet of fragrant dried herbs in a generous bow and hang the herbs on a cone wreath.

Wire small clusters of bleached wheat, natural wheat, and green rye grasses to a twig wreath that's been painted white, covering about a quarter of the wreath. Dry a dozen roses in silica gel, then wire clusters of the roses over the wheat. Next, coat the roses and the wheat with acrylic matte spray. To complete the wreath, tie a bow of white and ivory ribbon over the stems of the roses.

Festive Fare for Holiday Gatherings

It's the season of fellowship and good cheer, the time of the year when family and friends gather to share in the spirit of Christmas.

If you're planning a holiday gathering at your house this year, here are some appetizing options that are sure to make your celebration the toast of the town. All of the festive party fare you'll find on the next 12 pages is long on appeal but short on kitchen time. Mix and match finger foods and beverages as you like, but with an eye to an inviting array of colors and textures. Ideal for a holiday open house, these help-yourself foods will leave you plenty of time to enjoy the merrymaking.

Pictured clockwise, from top right, are *Spiced Orange Nog, Caraway-Sesame Flatbread, Nordic Dip, Mincemeat Fruitcake, Rosettes, Swiss Cheese Bites, Layered Vegetable Terrine, Make-Ahead Fruit Canapés, Coconut Tartlets,* and *Crème de Menthe Squares.*

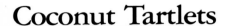

Coconut Tartlets

Pictured opposite.

1⅔ cups all-purpose flour
⅓ cup sugar
1 teaspoon finely shredded lime peel
¼ teaspoon salt
½ cup butter *or* margarine
1 slightly beaten egg
2 beaten eggs
½ cup sugar
¼ cup all-purpose flour
¼ teaspoon salt
¼ cup cream of coconut
2 tablespoons lime juice
2 tablespoons water
2 tablespoons butter *or* margarine, melted
2 cups coconut
¼ cup apple jelly *or* red currant jelly

In a mixing bowl stir together the 1⅔ cups flour, ⅓ cup sugar, lime peel, and ¼ teaspoon salt. Cut in the ½ cup butter or margarine till mixture resembles fine crumbs. Add the slightly beaten egg; stir till combined. Form dough into a ball. For *each* tartlet crust, pinch off *1 rounded teaspoon* of dough; press evenly onto bottom and sides of 1¾-inch muffin pans.

For filling, in a mixing bowl combine the 2 beaten eggs, ½ cup sugar, ¼ cup flour, and ¼ teaspoon salt. Add the cream of coconut, the lime juice, the water, and the 2 tablespoons melted butter or margarine; stir till combined. Stir in the coconut.

Spoon *1 rounded teaspoon* of the filling into *each* tartlet crust. Bake in a 325° oven about 25 minutes or till the pastry is golden and the filling is set.

Meanwhile, for glaze, in a small saucepan heat apple or currant jelly over low heat till melted. Brush the glaze onto hot tartlets. Cool on a wire rack; remove from pans. Makes 48 tartlets.

Make-Ahead Fruit Canapés

Almond Butter
Orange Aspic
30 slices firm-textured whole wheat *or* white bread
Assorted fruit and nut toppers*

Prepare Almond Butter and Orange Aspic. Cut crusts from whole wheat or white bread slices; trim slices to make squares. Spread about *2 tablespoons* of the Almond Butter onto *each* slice of bread. Spoon remaining Almond Butter into a decorating bag fitted with a star tip. For each buttered bread slice, pipe a border of Almond Butter onto 2 edges that are opposite each other.

Garnish each bread slice with small pieces of fruit or nuts. Slowly spoon about *2 teaspoons* of the partially set Orange Aspic over each fruit-topped slice to cover. Chill the bread slices in the refrigerator for 2 to 3 hours or till the aspic is firm. Before serving, cut each bread slice into 3 long triangles, so that the piped border is on the narrow side or base of the triangle. Makes 90 canapés.

*Note: Use small pieces of thinly sliced or cut-up fruits, such as unpeeled apples or pears, red or green seedless grapes, and grapefruit, orange, or mandarin orange sections. Treat apple and pear slices with lemon juice to keep the fruit from browning. For nuts, use broken pecans or walnuts, or use sliced almonds.

Almond Butter: Let two 8-ounce packages *cream cheese* and 1 cup *butter or margarine* stand at room temperature about 1 hour or till softened. In a large mixer bowl beat one 8-ounce can *almond paste* on medium speed of an electric mixer. Add cream cheese and butter or margarine; beat about 6 minutes or till fluffy.

Orange Aspic: In a small saucepan soften 1 envelope *unflavored gelatin* in ⅓ cup *cold water;* let stand for 5 minutes. Cook and stir over low heat till gelatin is dissolved. Remove from heat. Stir in ⅔ cup *cold water* and ⅓ cup *orange liqueur.* Chill in the refrigerator about 1 hour or to the consistency of unbeaten egg whites (partially set).

Crème de Menthe Squares

Pictured at right.

1¼ cups butter *or* margarine
½ cup unsweetened cocoa
    powder
3½ cups sifted powdered sugar
1 beaten egg
1 teaspoon vanilla
2 cups finely crushed graham
    crackers
⅓ cup green crème de menthe
1½ cups semisweet chocolate
    pieces

In a heavy saucepan combine ½ *cup* of the butter or margarine and the cocoa powder. Cook and stir over low heat till butter is melted. Remove from heat; stir in ½ cup of the powdered sugar, the egg, and the vanilla. Add graham crackers; stir till combined. Press onto the bottom of an ungreased 13x9x2-inch baking pan.

Melt ½ *cup* of the butter or margarine. In a mixer bowl combine the melted butter and crème de menthe. Gradually add the remaining powdered sugar, beating with an electric mixer till smooth. Spread over the chocolate layer. Chill in the refrigerator for 1 hour. In a heavy small saucepan combine the remaining ¼ cup butter or margarine and chocolate pieces. Cook and stir over low heat till melted. Spread over mint layer. Cover and chill for 1 to 2 hours or till firm. Cut into small squares. Store in the refrigerator. Makes about 96 squares.

Spiced Orange Nog

6 eggs
¼ cup sugar
1 quart vanilla ice cream,
    softened
¼ teaspoon ground
    cardamom
¼ teaspoon ground cinnamon
6 cups orange juice
    Orange Ice Ring (optional)
1 32-ounce bottle (1 quart)
    ginger ale, chilled

In a mixer bowl beat eggs on low speed of an electric mixer till combined. Gradually add sugar, beat-ing on medium speed till sugar is dissolved. Add the softened ice cream, cardamom, and cinnamon; beat on low speed till combined. Stir in orange juice. Cover; chill in the refrigerator till serving time. If desired, prepare Orange Ice Ring.

Before serving, transfer chilled mixture to a large punch bowl. Gradually add the ginger ale, stirring the mixture with an up-and-down motion. Float ice ring atop, if desired. Makes about 22 (6-ounce) servings.

Orange Ice Ring: Line the bottom of a ring mold with orange slices. Fill ring mold with enough water to cover; freeze till firm.

47

Nordic Dip

1 3¾-ounce can sardines in
   mustard sauce
1 3-ounce package cream
   cheese, softened
3 tablespoons chopped
   pimiento
1 teaspoon prepared
   horseradish
1 teaspoon Dijon-style
   mustard
½ teaspoon Worcestershire
   sauce
1 small clove garlic, minced
1 8-ounce carton plain
   yogurt
   Assorted vegetable dippers

In a blender container or food
processor bowl combine *undrained*
sardines, cream cheese, *1 tablespoon*
of the pimiento, horseradish, Dijon-style mustard, Worcestershire
sauce, and garlic. Blend or process
till smooth; stir into yogurt. Stir in
the remaining pimiento. Cover
and chill. Serve with vegetable
dippers. Makes 1½ cups.

Caraway-Sesame Flatbread

1 16-ounce loaf frozen
   whole wheat bread
   dough, thawed
1 beaten egg
2 tablespoons sesame seed
2 tablespoons caraway seed

Place the thawed dough into a
greased bowl; cover. Let rise till
double (about 1¾ hours). Divide
dough into 25 to 30 balls. Cover;
let rest for 5 minutes. Chill till
ready to bake. To bake, on a lightly floured surface roll each ball
into a 4½- to 5-inch paper-thin circle; place onto a greased baking
sheet. Combine egg and 1 tablespoon *water;* brush onto each circle. Combine sesame and caraway
seed; sprinkle about ½ *teaspoon*
seed atop each. Bake in a 350°
oven for 8 to 10 minutes or till
golden and crisp; cool on a rack.
Makes 25 to 30.

Rosettes

2 beaten eggs
1 cup all-purpose flour
1 cup milk
1 tablespoon sugar
1 teaspoon vanilla
   Cooking oil for deep-fat
    frying
   Powdered sugar

Combine eggs, flour, milk, sugar,
vanilla, and ¼ teaspoon *salt;* beat
till smooth. Heat a rosette iron in
deep hot oil (375°). Dip iron into
batter for 2 to 3 seconds (batter
should come three-fourths of the

way up the side of the iron). Dip
iron into hot oil for 30 to 45 seconds or till golden. Lift out; tip
slightly to drain. With a fork, push
rosette off iron onto paper towels
over a wire rack. Repeat with remaining batter, reheating the iron
each time. Sprinkle with powdered sugar. Makes 42.

Swiss Cheese Bites

3 cups shredded process
   Swiss cheese (12 ounces)
⅔ cup shortening
1½ cups all-purpose flour
3 tablespoons cold water

Bring cheese to room temperature. In a mixer bowl combine
cheese and shortening; beat on
medium speed of an electric mixer
till nearly smooth. Stir in flour.
Sprinkle *1 teaspoon* of the water
over part of the mixture; toss with
a fork. Push to side of bowl. Repeat till all is moistened. Shape
into 1-inch balls or 1½x½-inch
sticks. Place on a lightly greased
baking sheet. Bake in a 375° oven
for 20 to 25 minutes or till light
brown. Cool on wire racks. Makes
about 60.

Mincemeat Fruitcake

2 cups prepared mincemeat
2 cups diced mixed candied
  fruits and peels
  (16 ounces)
1 cup chopped walnuts
2½ cups all-purpose flour
½ teaspoon baking powder
½ teaspoon baking soda
¼ teaspoon salt
¼ cup butter *or* margarine
¾ cup packed brown sugar
1 teaspoon vanilla
2 eggs
  Brandy *or* bourbon *or* fruit
  juice
  Brandy Icing

Grease and lightly flour a 10-inch fluted tube pan; set pan aside. In a mixing bowl combine the mincemeat, candied fruits and peels, and walnuts; set aside. Stir together the flour, baking powder, baking soda, and salt.

In a large mixer bowl beat the butter or margarine on medium speed of an electric mixer for 30 seconds. Add the brown sugar and the vanilla; beat till fluffy. Add the eggs, one at a time, beating well on medium speed. Stir the dry ingredients into the beaten mixture (batter will be stiff). Stir in the fruit mixture.

Turn the batter into the prepared pan. Bake in a 325° oven about 65 minutes or till cake tests done. Cool thoroughly on a wire rack; remove from the pan. Wrap the cake in brandy-, bourbon-, or fruit-juice-moistened cheesecloth. Overwrap with foil. Store in a cool, dry place for at least 1 week.

Before serving, prepare Brandy Icing; drizzle over cake. Garnish with additional *candied fruit*, if desired. Slice thinly to serve. Makes 1 fruitcake.

Brandy Icing: In a small mixing bowl combine 1 cup sifted *powdered sugar*, 1 tablespoon *brandy or bourbon*, and ½ teaspoon *vanilla*. Add enough *milk* (1 to 2 tablespoons) to make icing of drizzling consistency.

Layered Vegetable Terrine

8 ounces chopped carrots
1 medium head romaine
1 large onion, finely chopped
  (1 cup)
1 4-ounce can chopped
  mushrooms, drained and
  finely chopped
1 clove garlic, minced
2 tablespoons butter *or*
  margarine
2 vegetable bouillon cubes,
  crushed
1 15-ounce can navy beans,
  drained
1½ cups soft bread crumbs
  (2 slices)
3 beaten eggs
½ cup butter *or* margarine,
  softened
3 bay leaves
½ teaspoon finely shredded
  lemon peel
1 tablespoon lemon juice
1 teaspoon dried savory,
  crushed

Cook carrots in boiling water for 10 to 15 minutes or till tender. Drain; set aside. Clean romaine and remove large stem. Reserve a few inner leaves; finely chop remaining leaves. Cook in a small amount of boiling salted water about 3 minutes or till crisp-tender. Drain well; squeeze out excess liquid. Measure 1 cup romaine. Cook onion, mushrooms, and garlic in 2 tablespoons butter till tender. Remove from heat. Dissolve bouillon in 2 tablespoons *hot water*. Mash beans. Stir bouillon, beans, crumbs, and ¼ teaspoon *pepper* into onion mixture. Stir in eggs and the ½ cup butter.

Place 2 of the bay leaves in a well-greased 8x4x2-inch loaf dish; crush the remaining leaf. Divide bean mixture in half. To halve, stir in carrots, lemon peel, and lemon juice; press into bottom of pan. To the remaining half, stir in cooked romaine, crushed bay leaf, and savory. Spoon atop carrot mixture; cover. Set into a 13x9x2-inch baking pan in the oven. Pour hot water into pan to a depth of 1 inch. Bake in a 350° oven about 1½ hours or till set. Cool; cover and chill for 2 hours. Before serving, let stand for 20 minutes at room temperature. Unmold the terrine onto a plate; trim with reserved romaine. Makes 1.

Layered Cheese And Pesto

Pictured opposite.

Pesto Filling (see
   recipe, right)
1 8-ounce package cream
   cheese
1 4½-ounce round
   Camembert *or* Brie
   cheese, rind removed
½ cup whipping cream
   Paprika (optional)
   Fresh basil
   Assorted crackers *or*
   French bread

Prepare the Pesto Filling. Set it aside. Bring the cream cheese and Camembert or Brie to room temperature. In a small mixer bowl beat cheeses together with an electric mixer till nearly smooth.

In a small mixing bowl beat the whipping cream till soft peaks form (tips curl). By hand, fold the whipped cream into cheese mixture.

Line a 3½- to 4-cup mold with clear plastic wrap. Spread ¼ of the cheese mixture into the prepared mold. Spread ⅓ of the Pesto Filling over cheese mixture. Repeat cheese and pesto layers 2 more times. Spread remaining cheese mixture on top. Cover and chill for several hours or overnight.

Before serving, invert the mold onto a serving plate. Remove the mold and carefully peel off the plastic wrap. Sprinkle with paprika, if desired. Garnish with basil. Serve with crackers or thin slices of French bread. Makes 3½ cups.

Pesto Filling

If fresh basil is hard to come by, increase the amount of snipped parsley to 1½ cups, and add 1 teaspoon dried basil, crushed.

1 cup snipped fresh basil,
   firmly packed
¾ cup grated Parmesan *or*
   Romano cheese
½ cup snipped parsley, firmly
   packed
¼ cup pine nuts, walnuts, *or*
   almonds
2 cloves garlic, quartered
⅓ cup olive oil *or* cooking oil

In a blender container or food processor bowl combine the basil, cheese, parsley, nuts, and garlic. Cover and process with several on/off turns till a paste forms. (Stop the machine occasionally to scrape down sides.) With machine running slowly, gradually add oil, and process to the consistency of soft butter. Makes about 1 cup.

Edam Cheese Spread

1 2¼- to 2½-pound block
   Edam cheese
¾ cup beer
¾ cup milk
¼ cup margarine *or* butter,
   softened
2 teaspoons caraway seed
2 teaspoons dry mustard
½ teaspoon celery salt
   Assorted fresh fruit pieces
   Assorted crackers
   Caraway seed (optional)

For round cheese, cut a thin slice from the top of the cheese. (For rectangular cheese, cut the block about 5 inches from 1 end.) Using a sharp knife, cut the sides of the block to make a scalloped edge. If necessary, cut a thin slice off the bottom to make the shell sit flat. With a spoon, scoop out cheese, leaving a ½- to 1-inch-thick shell. Wrap the shell and chill. Finely shred scooped-out cheese (about 7 cups). Soften shredded cheese, covered, at room temperature for 3 to 4 hours.

In a mixer bowl combine the cheese, beer, milk, margarine, caraway seed, mustard, and celery salt. Beat with an electric mixer for 3 to 5 minutes or till well combined. Fill reserved cheese shell with cheese spread. Sprinkle with caraway seed. Serve with fruit and crackers. Makes 4½ cups.

To make ahead, tightly wrap with clear plastic wrap. Store in the refrigerator. Remove and let stand at room temperature for 3 to 4 hours before serving.

Rose Hip Punch

You can buy dried rose hips for the punch, pictured opposite, in most health food stores.

8 cups water
4 cups fresh rose hips *or*
    2 cups dried rose hips
2 cups sugar
6 inches stick cinnamon
4 whole cloves
½ teaspoon ground nutmeg
2 cups white *or* rosé wine

In a large kettle combine the water, rose hips, sugar, cinnamon, cloves, and nutmeg. Simmer, covered, for 1 hour.

    Mash the rose hips with a potato masher while cooking. Cool mixture slightly and strain through a cheesecloth-lined strainer. Add white or rosé wine. Serve warm. Makes 16 (4-ounce) servings.

    Note: If using dried rose hips, increase water to 9 cups.

Spiced Party Punch

⅓ cup sugar
12 inches stick cinnamon, broken
½ teaspoon whole cloves
½ cup water
3 cups apple juice, chilled
1 12-ounce can apricot nectar, chilled
¼ cup lemon juice
2 1-liter bottles lemon-lime *or* grapefruit carbonated beverage, chilled
    Ice *or* ice ring

For syrup, in a small saucepan, combine sugar, cinnamon, cloves, and water; bring to boiling. Reduce heat; cover and simmer for 10 minutes. Strain out spices and discard. Chill. In a punch bowl combine sugar syrup with apple juice, apricot nectar, and lemon juice. Slowly pour in carbonated beverage; stir gently to mix. Add ice. Makes 22 (4-ounce) servings.

Spiced White Wine Punch: Prepare Spiced Party Punch as directed above, *except* omit carbonated beverage. Gently pour in two 750-milliliter bottles of chilled *dry white wine.* Stir to mix. Makes 23 (4-ounce) servings.

Spiked Party Punch: Prepare Spiced Party Punch as directed above, *except* omit carbonated beverage. In a punch bowl combine syrup mixture with apple juice, apricot nectar, lemon juice, and 2 cups *vodka, bourbon, brandy, or rum.* Stir to mix well. Makes 14 (4-ounce) servings.

Hot Buttered Cider

Let the cider stay warm for hours in a crockery cooker on low-heat setting.

8½ cups apple cider *or* apple juice
¼ cup packed brown sugar
4 inches stick cinnamon
1 teaspoon whole allspice
1 teaspoon whole cloves
    Peel of 1 lemon, cut into strips
    Butter *or* margarine

In a large saucepan combine cider or apple juice and brown sugar. Tie the cinnamon, allspice, cloves, and lemon peel in a cheesecloth bag. Add to saucepan. Bring to boiling, then reduce heat. Simmer, uncovered, for 15 minutes. Remove and discard spice bag. Ladle the cider into mugs and float about *½ teaspoon* butter or margarine atop each. Makes about 10 (6-ounce) servings.

Hot Buttered Rum and Cider: Prepare Hot Buttered Cider as directed above, except use 7 cups apple cider or apple juice; increase brown sugar to ⅓ cup. Stir in 1 to 1½ cups rum after removing spice bag.

Spiced Wassail

3 small cooking apples
½ cup brandy
¼ cup packed brown sugar
6 inches stick cinnamon, broken
½ teaspoon whole cloves
½ teaspoon whole allspice, crushed
3¼ cups dry red wine
1½ cups dry sherry

Core apples; peel strips around tops. Place into an 8x8x2-inch baking dish. Combine brandy and brown sugar. Bring to boiling. Pour over apples. Cover with foil. Bake in a 350° oven for 35 to 40 minutes or till tender. Drain, reserving ¾ cup of the syrup.

In a saucepan combine reserved syrup and ½ cup *water*. Tie spices in a cheesecloth bag; add to pan. Bring to boiling; reduce the heat. Cover; simmer for 10 minutes. Stir in wine and sherry. Heat through. Remove spice bag. Pour mixture into a heatproof punch bowl. Float apples atop. Pour into 12 heatproof glasses or cups. Garnish each serving with a cinnamon stick, if desired. Makes 12 (4-ounce) servings.

Cranberry Punch

1 cup boiling water
1 3-ounce package raspberry-flavored gelatin
1 6-ounce can frozen lemonade concentrate
3 cups cold water
1 32-ounce bottle cranberry juice cocktail, chilled
1 1-liter bottle grapefruit carbonated beverage, chilled
Ice ring *or* ice

Pour boiling water over gelatin; stir to dissolve. Stir in lemonade concentrate. Pour into a large punch bowl. Stir in cold water and cranberry juice cocktail. Slowly pour in grapefruit beverage; stir gently to mix. Add ice ring or ice. Makes 24 (4-ounce) servings.

Minted Fruit Punch

1 teaspoon dried mint leaves
½ cup honey
1 cup orange juice
1 cup grape juice
¾ cup lemon juice
2 cups chilled carbonated water
Lemon and orange slices

Combine 1½ cups *boiling water* and mint leaves; let stand for 5 minutes. Stir in honey. Add orange, grape, and lemon juices. Cover and chill. To serve, strain the mixture through several thicknesses of cheesecloth; stir in carbonated water. Garnish with fruit slices. Makes 8 (7-ounce) servings.

Elegant Syllabub

Pictured opposite.

½ cup sugar
1 cup dry white wine, chilled
2 teaspoons finely shredded lemon peel
3 tablespoons lemon juice
1½ cups milk
1 cup light cream
Freshly grated nutmeg
2 egg whites
2 tablespoons sugar

Stir together ½ cup sugar, wine, lemon peel, and juice till sugar dissolves. In a large mixing bowl combine milk, cream, and wine mixture. Beat with a rotary beater till smooth and frothy. Pour into a punch bowl; top with nutmeg.

In a mixer bowl beat egg whites with 2 tablespoons sugar till stiff peaks form (tips stand straight). Spoon puffs of egg white on the syllabub. Ladle syllabub into glasses; serve with spoons. Makes 8 (½-cup) servings.

Café Brûlot

Peel of 1 small orange
Peel of 1 lemon
6 medium sugar cubes
6 whole cloves
6 whole allspices
1 cinnamon stick, broken
½ cup brandy
2 cups hot strong coffee

Cut the lemon and orange peel in thin slivers. Place the peels, sugar, and spices in a chafing dish pan. In a saucepan warm the brandy. Pour ⅓ cup of the brandy into chafing dish. Put the remaining brandy into a long-handled ladle with a deep bowl (leave the remaining brandy in the saucepan if a suitable ladle is not available). Ignite brandy in ladle with a long match; carefully pour into chafing dish. Dip and pour flaming brandy over sugar cubes so they burn and melt. Gradually add the coffee; continue to ladle the mixture until the flame dies. Ladle immediately into demitasse cups. Makes 8 servings.

White Wine Sangria

½ lemon, chilled and thinly sliced
½ orange, chilled and thinly sliced
½ apple, chilled and thinly sliced
1 750-milliliter bottle dry white wine, chilled
¼ cup brandy
1 tablespoon sugar
1 12-ounce can lemon-lime carbonated beverage, chilled

In a 1½-quart pitcher combine lemon, orange, and apple slices. Add wine, brandy, and sugar; stir till sugar is dissolved. Slowly pour carbonated beverage down the side of the pitcher. Stir gently with an up-and-down motion to mix. Serve immediately in wineglasses. Makes 8 (6-ounce) servings.

Red Wine Sangria

2 oranges
2 lemons *or* limes
¼ cup sugar
1 750-milliliter bottle dry red wine *or* rosé wine, chilled
2 cups carbonated water, chilled

Cut 1 orange and 1 lemon into slices. Squeeze juice from remaining fruits into a 1½-quart pitcher; stir in sugar. Stir in wine. Slowly pour the carbonated water down the side of the pitcher. Stir gently with an up-and-down motion to mix. Add fruit slices. Serve immediately in wineglasses. Makes 8 (6-ounce) servings.

Soft-Cider Lamb's Wool

4 large cooking apples
2 quarts apple cider
¼ cup packed brown sugar
2 teaspoons pickling spice
12 cinnamon sticks

Wrap each apple in foil; place on a baking sheet. Bake in a 425° oven about 1 hour or until very soft. Scrape pulp from skins and chop coarsely or puree in a food mill.

In a large saucepan combine cider, sugar, and pickling spice. Bring to boiling; reduce heat and simmer about 10 minutes. Strain mixture through cheesecloth to remove spice. Add apple pulp to cider. Serve in mugs, with a stick of cinnamon in each for stirring. Makes 12 (½-cup) servings.

Colonial Tavern Flip

Pictured at right.

1 quart ale or beer
4 eggs
¼ cup sugar
1 teaspoon ground ginger
½ teaspoon freshly grated
    nutmeg
¼ cup dark rum

Heat ale to boiling. Beat eggs with a rotary beater or electric mixer. Add sugar and spices; beat well. Pour egg mixture into a pitcher. Pour ale into a heatproof pitcher; add rum. Add a little ale mixture to egg mixture, stirring briskly so it does not curdle; add remaining ale. Pour mixture back and forth between two pitchers till smooth and foamy. Makes 12 (½-cup) servings.

Kentucky Bourbon Eggnog

6 eggs, separated
¾ cup sugar
2 cups milk
½ cup bourbon
¼ cup dark rum
2 cups whipping cream,
    whipped
   Freshly grated nutmeg

In a small mixer bowl beat egg yolks well with an electric mixer; add ½ cup of the sugar and beat till thick. Stir in the milk, bourbon, and rum. Cover and chill.

Beat the egg whites till frothy. Gradually add the remaining sugar; beat till soft peaks form. Fold egg whites and whipped cream into the yolk mixture. Serve cold sprinkled with nutmeg. Makes 24 (½-cup) servings.

Snowflake Punch

3 quarts vanilla ice cream
2 cups bourbon
1 cup light rum
   Strawberry Ice Ring
   (optional)
14 cups milk

In a mixing bowl stir ice cream *just till softened.* Stir in bourbon and rum; freeze in 2 portions. Prepare Strawberry Ice Ring, if desired. Before serving, turn the frozen mixture into a large punch bowl. Gradually stir in milk. Float the ice ring atop, if desired. Makes about 34 (6-ounce) servings.

Strawberry Ice Ring: Combine one 10-ounce package frozen sliced *strawberries,* thawed, with enough *water* to fill a ring mold. Pour the berry mixture into the ring mold and freeze about 6 hours or till firm. To serve, unmold the ice ring and float it atop the punch.

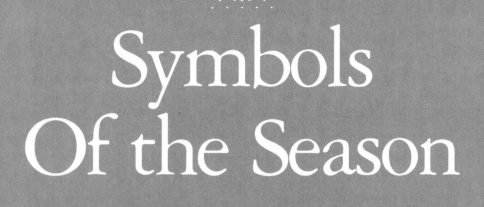

Symbols
Of the Season

Star for a Day

As a child, I believed that no matter how many Christmas traditions my family had in our home in the Green Bay, Wisconsin, area, they were never enough. A stunner of a tree was the backdrop for the lavish Christmas dinners we staged, the table set with Spode china and long-stemmed crystal goblets. The turkey on its huge platter was surrounded by an impressive array of relishes and vegetables in silver dishes.

But still, I longed for a truly dramatic tradition, preferably with costume. Elements of glamour, even danger, were needed. Our family history had no tradition of this sort, but being a greedy child, I was not content with the beautiful Christmases that my parents gave us.

I began to cast about among my friends to find a suitable ritual. I discovered what I wanted when I talked to a Swedish girl. She had long fair hair and the eyes of an angel. She, as the youngest in a family of four, was to be Santa Lucia on December 13.

Santa Lucia is the saint of light. I was impressed to learn that she was an early Christian martyr whose eyes were gouged out with hot pokers by Roman guards. Miraculously, however, perfect sight was restored to her. Her feast day is December 13. She comes on that day to announce the beginning of Christmas and the lengthening of days.

My friend's mother was making her a long white gown. She would wear a wreath of cranberries (in lieu of lingonberries) in her hair.

Fixed in the wreath were seven lighted candles. On December 13 she would get up before dawn, put on all the regalia, and wake each member of the family with a cup of coffee and rolls called *lussekatter.* Star for a day.

It was wearing those lighted candles that sold me. I determined I'd introduce this tradition into our household. I'd figure out how to make the rolls and coffee, get an old sheet, and make myself a gown. Surely it couldn't be more difficult than those togas we made for Latin Club. I, too, could be star for a day and surprise my family.

The problem was that my father would be away on business on December 13, so I decided on a new feast day for Santa Lucia—Christmas day. (Tradition, according to the Swedish girl, dictated that Santa Lucia should be played by the youngest girl in the family. I was the oldest of three girls; my youngest sister was 5 at the time. Surely Mother would be horrified to see her with lighted candles in her hair, I reasoned. I had to take on this awesome responsibility myself.)

On Christmas Eve afternoon, while my parents were off on secret errands, I made the rolls. Something went wrong. When I pulled them from the oven they looked like brown stones.

So much for that. I'd use some of our large supply of Christmas cookies. Surely anyone would rather have frosted sugar cookies for breakfast than boring old rolls. I'd add a hard-boiled egg for each member of the family, and Mother couldn't complain about an unbalanced breakfast.

That night we got to bed very late, having sung carols around the piano with Mother playing my father's favorite, "O Little Town of Bethlehem" any number of times. Too many times, I thought. I had my mind on my last-minute preparations.

I stored everything under my bed: the candles, a wreath of artificial leaves from one of my mother's old hats, cranberries to drape around it, the gown, and the food. The last thing I did was to set my alarm to ring at five.

I awoke with my little sisters tickling my feet, begging me to get up. I looked at the clock. It was seven-thirty. I could hear my parents talking in the kitchen downstairs. I took one last look under my bed; the accoutrements of stardom were still there. But whatever visions I had of Santa Lucia slowly mounting the stairs, the house dark except for seven glowing candles—emblems of sanctity—all vanished.

Outside, the day was gaining light. Beneath the Christmas tree was a mass of packages tied with red and gold satin ribbons. My mother appeared, carrying a tray filled with her own special orange rolls.

"Merry Christmas," she said. "I think you might be old enough for a cup of coffee. What do you think?"

I agreed. And in the kitchen pouring coffee for us three grownups, I saw that the way our own family celebrated Christmas—would probably always celebrate Christmas—was enough.

—Pauline W. Wanderer

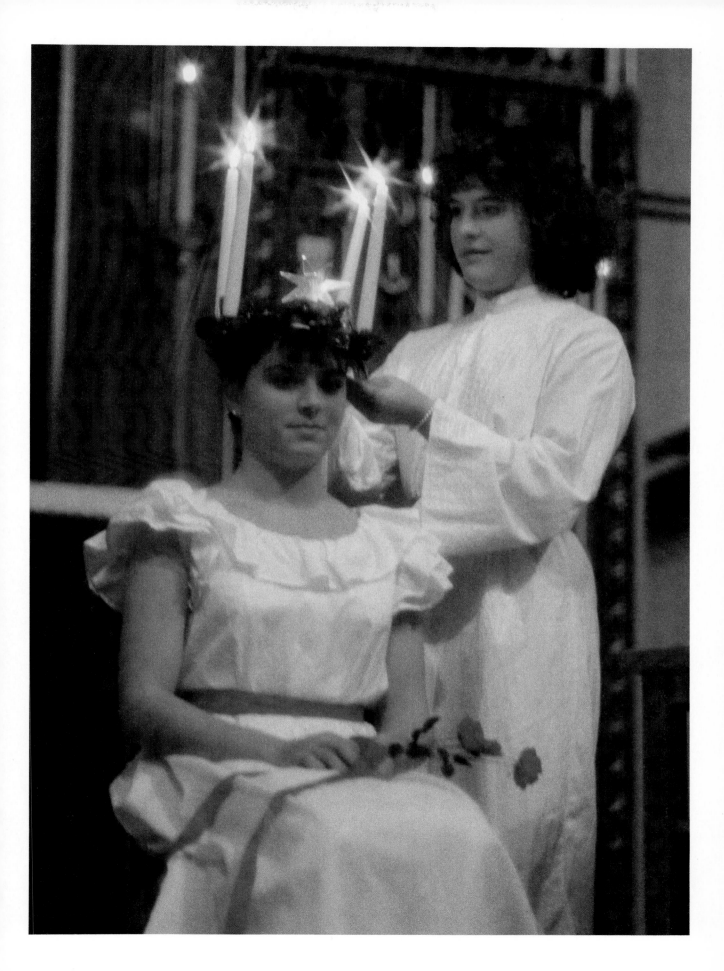

Carols in Gloucestershire

—Laurie Lee

Later, towards Christmas, there was heavy snow, which raised the roads to the top of the hedges. There were millions of tons of the lovely stuff, plastic, pure, all-purpose, which nobody owned, which no one could carve or tunnel, eat, or just throw about. It covered the hills and cut off the villages, but nobody thought of rescues; for there was hay in the barns and flour in the kitchens, the women baked bread, the cattle were fed and sheltered—we'd been cut off before, after all.

The week before Christmas, when snow seemed to lie thickest, was the moment for carol-singing; and when I think back to those nights it is to the crunch of snow and to the lights of the lanterns on it. Carol-singing in my village was a special tithe for the boys, the girls had little to do with it. Like hay-making, black-berrying, stone-clearing, and wishing-people-a-happy-Easter, it was one of our seasonal perks.

By instinct we knew just when to begin it; a day too soon and we should have been unwelcome, a day too late and we should have received lean looks from people whose bounty was already exhausted. When the true moment came, exactly balanced, we recognized it and were ready.

So as soon as the wood had been stacked in the oven to dry for the morning fire, we put on our scarves and went out through the streets, calling loudly between our hands, till the various boys who knew the signal ran out from their houses to join us.

One by one they came stumbling over the snow, swinging their lanterns around their heads, shouting and coughing horribly.

'Coming carol-barking then?'

We were the Church Choir, so no answer was necessary. For a year we had praised the Lord out of key, and as a reward for this service—on top of the Outing—we now had the right to visit all the big houses, to sing our carols and collect our tribute.

To work them all in meant a five-mile journey over wild and generally snowed-up country. So the first thing we did was to plan our route; a formality, as the route never changed. All the same, we blew on our fingers and argued; and then we chose our Leader. This was not binding, for we all fancied ourselves as Leaders, and he who started the night in that position usually trailed home with a bloody nose.

Eight of us set out that night. There was Sixpence the Simple, who had never sung in his life (he just worked his mouth in Church); the brothers Horace and Boney, who were always fighting everybody and always getting the worst of it; Clergy Green, the preaching maniac; Walt the bully, and my two brothers. As we went down the lane other boys, from other villages, were already about the hills, bawling 'Kingwenslush', and shouting through keyholes 'Knock on the knocker! Ring at the Bell! Give us a penny for singing so well!' They weren't an approved charity as we were, the Choir; but competition was in the air.

Our first call as usual was the house of the Squire, and we trouped nervously down his drive. For light we had candles in marmalade-jars suspended on loops of string, and they threw pale gleams on the towering snowdrifts that stood on each side of the drive. A blizzard was blowing, but we were well wrapped up, with Army puttees on our legs, woollen hats on our heads, and several scarves around our ears.

continued

As we approached the Big House across its white silent lawns, we too grew respectfully silent. The lake near by was stiff and black, the waterfall frozen and still. We arranged ourselves shuffling around the big front door, then knocked and announced the Choir.

A maid bore the tidings of our arrival away into the echoing distances of the house, and while we waited we cleared our throats noisily. Then she came back, and the door was left ajar for us, and we were bidden to begin. We brought no music, the carols were in our heads. 'Let's give 'em "Wild Shepherds",' said Jack. We began in confusion, plunging into a wreckage of keys, of different words and tempo; but we gathered our strength; he who sang loudest took the rest of us with him, and the carol took shape if not sweetness.

This huge stone house, with its ivied walls, was always a mystery to us. What were those gables, those rooms and attics, those narrow windows veiled by the cedar trees? As we sang 'Wild Shepherds' we craned our necks, gaping into that lamplit hall which we had never entered; staring at the muskets and untenanted chairs, the great tapestries furred by dust—until suddenly, on the stairs, we saw the old Squire himself standing and listening with his head on one side.

He didn't move until we'd finished; then slowly he tottered towards us, dropping two coins in our box with a trembling hand, scratched his name in the book we carried, gave us each a long look with his moist blind eyes, then turned away in silence.

As though released from a spell, we took a few sedate steps, then broke into a run for the gate. We didn't stop till we were out of the grounds. Impatient, at last, to discover the extent of his bounty, we squatted by cowsheds, held our lanterns over the book, and saw that he had written 'Two Shillings'. This was quite a good start. No one of any worth in the district would dare to give us less than the Squire.

So with money in the box, we pushed on up the valley, pouring scorn on each other's performance. Confident now, we began to consider our quality and whether one carol was not better suited to us than another. Horace, Walt said, shouldn't sing at all; his voice was beginning to break. Horace disputed this and there was a brief token battle—they fought as they walked, kicking up divots of snow, then they forgot it, and Horace still sang.

Steadily we worked through the length of the valley, going from house to house, visiting the lesser and the greater gentry—the farmers, the doctors, the merchants, the majors and other exalted persons. It was freezing hard and blowing too; yet not for a moment did we feel the cold. The snow blew into our faces, into our eyes and mouths, soaked through our puttees, got into our boots, and dripped from our woollen caps. But we did not care. The collecting-box grew heavier, and the list of names in the book longer and more extravagant, each trying to outdo the other.

Mile after mile we went, fighting against the wind, falling into snowdrifts, and navigating by the lights of the houses. And yet we never saw our audience. We called at house after house; we sang in courtyards and porches, outside windows, or in the damp gloom of hallways; we heard voices from hidden rooms; we smelt rich clothes and strange hot food; we saw maids bearing in dishes or carrying away coffee-cups; we received nuts, cakes, figs, preserved ginger, dates, cough-drops and money; but we never once saw our patrons. We sang as it were at the castle walls, and apart from the Squire, who had shown himself to prove that he was still alive, we never expected it otherwise.

As the night drew on there was trouble with Boney. 'Noël', for instance, had a rousing harmony which Boney persisted in singing, and singing flat. The others forbade him to sing it at all, and Boney said he would fight us. Picking himself up, he agreed we were right, then he disappeared altogether. He just turned away and walked into the snow and wouldn't answer when we called him back. Much later, as we reached a far point up the valley, somebody said 'Hark!' and we stopped to listen. Far away across the fields from the distant village came the sound of a frail voice singing, singing 'Noël', and singing it flat—it was Boney, branching out on his own.

We approached our last house high up on the hill, the place of Joseph the farmer. For him we had chosen a special carol, which was about the other Joseph, so that we always felt that singing it added a spicy cheek to the night. The last stretch of country to reach his farm was perhaps the most difficult of all. In these rough bare lanes, open to all winds, sheep were buried and wagons lost. Huddled together, we tramped in one another's footsteps, powdered snow blew into our screwed-up eyes, the candles burnt low, some blew out altogether, and we talked loudly above the gale.

Crossing, at last, the frozen mill-stream—whose wheel in summer still turned a barren mechanism—we climbed up to Joseph's farm. Sheltered by trees, warm on its bed of snow, it seemed always to be like this. As always it was late; as always this was our final call. The snow had a fine crust upon it, and the old trees sparkled like tinsel.

We grouped ourselves round the farmhouse porch. The sky cleared, and broad streams of stars ran down over the valley and away to Wales. On Slad's white slopes, seen through the black sticks of its woods, some red lamps still burned in the windows.

Everything was quiet; everywhere there was the faint crackling silence of the winter night. We started singing, and we were all moved by the words and the sudden trueness of our voices. Pure, very clear, and breathless we sang:

> *As Joseph was a-walking*
> *He heard an angel sing;*
> *'This night shall be the birth-time*
> *Of Christ the Heavenly King.*
>
> *He neither shall be borned*
> *In Housen nor in hall,*
> *Nor in a place of paradise*
> *But in an ox's stall. . . .'*

And 2,000 Christmasses became real to us then; the houses, the halls, the places of paradise had all been visited; the stars were bright to guide the Kings through the snow; and across the farmyard we could hear the beasts in their stalls. We were given roast apples and hot mince-pies, in our nostrils were spices like myrrh, and in our wooden box, as we headed back for the village, there were golden gifts for all.

—from Cider with Rosie

Toys and Togs
For Kids

On the following pages, you'll find gifts galore for the children on your Christmas list: a delightful doll, embroidered and appliquéd stockings, a cuddly teddy bear, colorful mittens, and the machine-appliquéd sweatshirts at left and opposite. Decorating an inexpensive sweatshirt with ma-

chine-appliquéd embellishments transforms it from ordinary sportswear into something special. The four motifs are cut from fabric and matching pieces of fusible webbing. After the fabric is affixed to the front of the sweatshirt, the raw edges are covered with rows of machine satin stitches.

Animal Sweatshirts

Shown on pages 66 and 67.

MATERIALS
Purchased sweatshirts
Fabric scraps in desired colors
½ yard each of medium-weight
 iron-on interfacing and fusible
 webbing (2 sweatshirts)
Threads to match fabrics
Tissue paper
Typing paper

INSTRUCTIONS
Wash and dry sweatshirts before stitching appliqués in place. Iron interfacing to backs of fabric scraps before cutting out appliqué shapes. Using tissue paper, trace around patterns on pages 68–71 for each shape to be appliquéd. Pin tissue paper pieces to desired fabrics and cut out; cut a matching piece of fusible webbing for each piece of fabric appliqué.

To fuse the appliqués, slip the shaped pieces of fusible webbing between the sweatshirt and the fabric appliqué pieces, then press the layers to the sweatshirt using a warm iron. *Note:* Slip paper towels between the iron and the fabric to catch stray wisps of the heated fusible webbing.

To stitch, place a sheet of typing paper inside the sweatshirt, under the area to be appliquéd. (This will keep the sweatshirt from stretching as you sew.) Using a wide, tight zigzag stitch, sew along raw edges of fabric cutouts, covering the edges completely with thread. Change thread colors in the machine to match the colors of the fabric.

Embroidered And Appliquéd Stockings

Finished size of stockings is 24 inches tall.

MATERIALS

(for both stockings)

Scraps of red and green fabrics for appliqués

¾ yard each of white fabric (stocking front and back) and lining fabric

25x28-inch piece of fleece for each stocking

⅓ yard of red piping for each stocking

White, red, yellow, green, and brown embroidery floss

Embroidery hoop and needle

Tiny red buttons; brown buttons; 3 yellow star buttons (optional)

Dressmaker's carbon paper

Tissue paper

Thread

INSTRUCTIONS

Enlarge the cuff and stocking patterns, *opposite,* onto tissue paper, adding ½-inch seam allowances all around.

CUFFS: Transfer the cuff pattern onto red fabric using dressmaker's carbon paper; do not cut out. Mount the fabric in a hoop, and embroider the design, using two strands of white floss. Cut out the cuff; cut a matching lining from red pindot fabric. Set the cuffs aside.

EMBROIDERED STOCKING: Enlarge the pattern, *opposite,* and transfer it to white fabric using dressmaker's carbon.

On stocking front, using three strands of green floss, work backstitches for circles, or sew red buttons in place. Backstitch garland stems and work lazy-daisy stitches for leaves.

Transfer the toe and heel patterns onto red print fabric, adding ¼ inch for seams; cut out. Turning under the raw edges, appliqué the toe and heel in place, then embroider the inner edges with double rows of yellow backstitches (see photograph, *above*).

For the pocket, transfer rectangle pattern (with the saying) onto green print fabric, adding ¼-inch seam allowances; do not cut out.

Using three strands of embroidery floss, backstitch the pocket outline with yellow. Work yellow running stitches just inside the outline; backstitch the letter outlines in red. Fill the letters with yellow satin stitches.

Cut out the pocket and matching green lining. With right sides facing, sew the pocket front to back, leaving an opening for turning. Turn, press, and sew the opening. Sew the star buttons in place. Sew pocket to stocking.

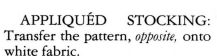

APPLIQUÉD STOCKING: Transfer the pattern, *opposite,* onto white fabric.

Cut apart the stocking design for the appliqué patterns. Cut the appliqués from the desired fabrics without adding seam allowances. Machine-satin-stitch the appliqués in place. Using brown floss and satin stitches, embroider the bear's eyes and nose; outline-stitch the bear's mouth. Sew small brown buttons in place for the bear's elbow and leg joints.

ASSEMBLY: Cut out the stocking front and back. Cut two stocking shapes from fleece. Baste the fleece to the wrong side of the stocking front and back; trim the fleece.

Sew the lining pieces together, right sides facing, leaving the top edge open. Trim seams and clip curves.

Sew the piping to the stocking front. Sew front to back with right sides facing, leaving the top edge open. Clip, turn, and press.

Sew together the short ends of the embroidered cuff; repeat for lining. Leaving the straight edge unstitched, sew the cuff to the lining (right sides facing). Clip curves, turn, and press.

With right sides facing, slip the cuff inside the stocking lining; sew the straight edges together. Trim seam, turn, and press.

Insert the lining/cuff into the stocking, wrong sides facing. Turn under the seam on the stocking top; sew the stocking to the lining. Turn the cuff to the outside of the stocking. Add a loop for hanging.

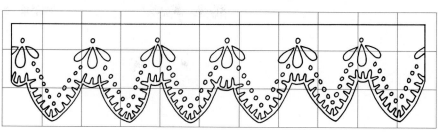

1 Square = 2 Inches

1 Square = 2 Inches

Stocking Song on Christmas Eve

Welcome Christmas! heel
   and toe,
Here we wait thee in a row.
Come, good Santa Claus,
   we beg
Fill us tightly, foot and leg.

Fill us quickly ere you go,—
Fill us till we overflow,
That's the way! and leave us
   more
Heaped in piles upon the
   floor.

—*Mary Mapes Dodge*

Country Doll

Finished doll is 18 inches tall.

MATERIALS
½ yard of muslin
½ yard of white printed fabric
½ yard of red paisley fabric
10 yards of off-white bulky
    yarn (hair)
One 2-inch square *each* of red
    and green fabric

4 inches of ⅛-inch-wide elastic
Thread; pink marker
White embroidery floss
No. 535 gray embroidery
    floss
9 inches of ecru piping
Polyester fiberfill; graph paper
Dressmaker's carbon paper

INSTRUCTIONS
Enlarge the pattern *opposite* onto graph paper. *Note:* Patterns include ¼-inch seams.

Cut pattern pieces as follows: body parts from muslin; dress bodice, sleeves, and a 10x16-inch apron front, two 1½x5-inch apron straps, and a 1½x12-inch waistband from red paisley.

FACE: First stitch the two face pieces, right sides together, along the center seam. Matching the center seam of fabric to center seam of pattern, transfer the embroidery lines to the face with dressmaker's carbon paper.

Embroider the eyes, the mouth, and the stitches along the center seam with two strands of gray floss and outline or stem stitches. Color the cheeks with a pink marker.

BODY/HEAD: On the front of the body, stitch the dart as indicated. With right sides together, match the neck edges of the chin to the face, right sides facing, matching the chin fold line to the center seam of the face. Stitch. With right sides facing, pin the two head and body pieces together along the center back seam; stitch. Sew the body/head back to the front, right sides facing, easing curves and leaving the bottom open. Clip curves and trim seams. Turn the body right side out and stuff it firmly. Sew bottom closed.

ARMS AND HEAD: Sew the arm and leg backs to the fronts, right sides together, and stitch, leaving the top of each open. Trim seams, clip curves, and turn inside out. Stuff and slip-stitch openings closed. Sew the arms and legs to the body where indicated on the pattern.

HAIR: Cut the yarn into 6-inch lengths. Separate the lengths into eight bunches, then wrap thread around the center of each bunch and tack to the head.

DRESS: Sew the bodice and sleeve pieces together along the shoulders and underarms, right sides facing. Slash the back along the length of the fold line.

Fold under ¼ inch on the raw edges of the bottoms of the sleeves and tuck a 2-inch length of

elastic under the seam allowance on each. Pulling the elastic taut while you sew, stitch through the seam allowance and elastic. This will gather the bottoms of the sleeves. Sew the short sides of the skirt together, right sides facing, leaving the seam open 2 inches at one end. This seam will be the center back seam, and the opening will be at the top of the back.

Center the waistband strip over the apron front, right sides together. Stitch. Fold under the raw edges of the waistband; press. Wrap the waistband around the doll and tack in place, catching the doll in the stitches. Fold the raw edges of the shoulder straps to the inside along the long edges; press. Topstitch close to the edges of the straps. Then position the straps

over the doll's shoulders, tucking the ends under the waistband in the front and back. Stitch.

Hem the skirt bottom and gather the top edge to fit the bodice waist. With right sides facing, sew the skirt to the bodice, matching the back openings. Trim the bodice neck with ecru piping. Put the dress on the doll and sew the back openings closed, tucking raw edges inside and catching the back of the doll in the stitches.

APRON: Finish the short sides of the apron front with rolled hems and stitch a 1-inch hem along one long edge. Using white floss and long, straight stitches, sew the fabric-square patches to the apron front. Gather the upper edge of the apron front until it is 5 inches long.

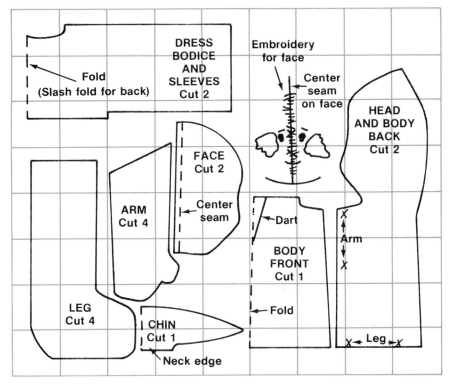

1 Square = 2 Inches

Teddy Bear

Bear is 21 inches tall.

MATERIALS
¾ yard of baby-wale brown
  corduroy
1 square of pink felt (inner
  ears, cheeks, hand and foot
  pads)
Scrap of tan felt (outer eye,
  nose)
Scrap of brown felt (inner eye)
Embroidery floss in tan and
  white
Polyester fiberfill
Beanbag pellets
Tissue paper
Dental floss
1½ yards of 1-inch-wide
  ribbon

INSTRUCTIONS
Note: The patterns include a ¼-
inch seam allowance unless otherwise noted. Sew all seams twice,
using small stitches and with right
sides facing. Use dental floss to
sew openings closed and to sew
head and limbs to body.

Trace the patterns, *opposite.* Enlarge the patterns onto tissue paper. Cut patterns from fabrics as
indicated in the materials list.

BODY: Sew center fronts together, then sew center backs together. Clip curves. Sew front to back at sides. Sew base to body, matching sides and center; clip and turn. Set aside.

ARMS: Topstitch the hand pads to the arms, reversing placement. Sew arms together in pairs, leaving tops open; clip and turn. Stuff, leaving tops of arms unstuffed. Sew arms to neck sides, matching raw edges. Stuff body with pellets, leaving an empty space at top of body.

HEAD: Sew center backs together. Sew front darts; trim. Sew forehead to each head side from A to B. Sew center fronts together from B to C. Sew front to back; clip, turn, and stuff. Use floss to hand-sew across base of head, holding stuffing in place.

LEGS: Topstitch the edge of the pads to the leg backs, reversing placement.

Sew darts; clip instep dart and trim remaining darts. Layer legs together in pairs, with leg front on top. Sew from A to B. Break stitching; fold darts toward leg top. Sew from C to D. Break

stitching again; fold darts toward toe. Sew from E to F.

Clip, turn, and stuff feet firmly with fiberfill; use beanbag pellets for leg tops, allowing an empty space at the tops. Turn raw edges in and whipstitch closed. Sew legs to front of body base.

FACE: Hand-sew the eyes, nose, and cheeks to the face. Use three strands of floss to chain-stitch the smile, straight-stitch the eyelashes, and outline-stitch the eyebrows. Topstitch edge of inner ears to ears.

Tie a ribbon into a bow around the bear's neck.

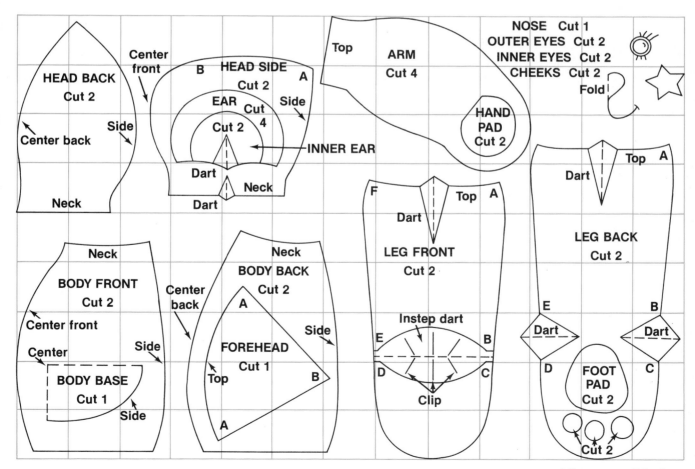

1 Square = 2 Inches

Two-Needle Mittens

Directions are for size Small. Changes for Medium and Large follow in parentheses. Finished measurement around palm above thumb = 5¼ (6¼, 7) inches.

MATERIALS

1 skein of worsted-weight yarn in the desired color for each pair of mittens
Sizes 6 and 8 knitting needles or size to obtain gauge below.
Small amount of contrasting yarn for embroidery
Stitch holder; tapestry needle

Gauge: With larger needle over st st 9 sts = 2 inches.

INSTRUCTIONS

With smaller needles cast on 24 (28, 32) sts. Work in k 1, p 1 rib until length measures 2 (2½, 2¾) inches.

Change to larger needles and st st; work even for 4 (4, 6) rows.

Divide for thumb gusset: K 11 (13, 15), place marker, inc in each of next 2 sts, place marker, k 11 (13, 15).

Next row: Purl. Continue to inc after first marker and before second marker every other row until there are 12 (12, 14) sts bet markers; end with wrong-side row—34 (38, 44) sts.

Next row: K 12 (14, 16) and sl these sts to holder, k next 10 (10, 12) sts for thumb; sl rem 12 (14, 16) sts to second holder.

Working on 10 (10, 12) thumb sts, cast on 1 st at beg of next row and work even until length of thumb measures ¾ (1, 1¼) inch-(es). End with wrong-side row—11 (11, 13) sts.

THUMB SHAPING: (K 1, k 2 tog) 3 (3, 4) times, end k 2 (2, 1)—8 (8, 9) sts.

Next row: Purl.

Next row: K 2 tog around; *size Large only:* end k 1—4 (4, 5) sts.

Break off, leaving tail for sewing thumb seam.

Thread needle and pull tail through rem sts; pull tightly, fasten, and sew thumb seam.

Sl 24 (28, 32) sts from holders to needle. Continue in st st until length from beg of st st above rib measures 3½ (4, 4½) inches.

TOP SHAPING: Row 1—K 1, k 2 tog, k 6 (8, 10), k 2 tog, k 2, k 2 tog, k 6 (8, 10), k 2 tog, k 1—20 (24, 28) sts.

Row 2: Purl.

Row 3: K 1, k 2 tog, k 4 (6, 8), k 2 tog, k 2, k 2 tog, k 4, (6, 8), k 2 tog, k 1—16 (20, 24) sts.

Row 4: Purl.

Row 5: K 1, k 2 tog, k 2 (4, 6), k 2 tog, k 2, k2 tog, k 2 (4, 6), k 2 tog, k 1—12 (16, 20) sts.

Row 6: Purl.

Row 7: K 2 tog across—6 (8, 10) sts. Break off, leaving tail long

enough to sew side seam. Thread tapestry needle; draw tail through rem sts; pull tightly and fasten.

Decorate mittens as directed below. Sew side seam.

VARIATIONS: *Red and white striped mittens*—Work st st as follows: Work 4 rows white and 2 rows red; rep these 6 rows for stripe pat.

White mittens with red and green polka dots: Knit white mittens. Beg with the first row of st st, work green duplicate st every fourth st. Rep every fourth row, alternating rows of red and green duplicate sts and placing duplicate sts at midpoint between duplicate sts of previous row.

Red mittens with embroidered flowers: Work white French knots for flowers and green straight sts for stems and leaves.

Red and green striped mittens: Work green cuff, then work 4 rows red, 4 rows green; rep these last 8 rows for stripe pat.

Red mittens with white snowflake: With white yarn, make a 2-inch upright cross in center of mitten. Make a 1¼-inch diagonal cross over first cross. Work small V ¼ inch from tip of upright cross.

Green mittens with white striped cuff: Cast on in green. Work 2 rows rib in green, then 2 rows rib in white. Rep these 4 rows twice more to complete cuff. Finish mitten with green.

Red and white striped mittens with green dots: Make white cuff. Work 3 rows st st with white. Work 1 row red. Continue this 4-row stripe pattern to end of mitten. Embroider 3 green French knots, centering on white stripe above first red stripe. Rep knots every white stripe, placing at midpoint bet knots of previous row.

Heart Mittens

Directions are for size Small. Changes for sizes Medium and Large follow in parentheses. Finished measurement around hand above
thumb = 6¼ (6½, 7½) inches.

MATERIALS
Red Heart Wintuk knitting (3½-ounce skein): 1 skein *each* of No. 902 jockey and No. 1 white.
Size 4 knitting needles
1 set of Size 4 double-pointed needles or size to obtain gauge given below.
Tapestry needle; bobbins

Gauge: Over st st 5 sts = 1 inch.

INSTRUCTIONS
Note on two-color knitting: When changing yarn colors, always twist new color around color in use to avoid making holes. Do not carry unused color loosely across back; use bobbins instead.

Beg at cuff, with single-pointed needles and red, cast on 31 (33, 37) sts.

K 1, * p 1, k 1; rep from * across. Continue in rib as established until 10 (16, 18) rows are completed.

Change to st st and work even 2 (6, 8) rows, ending with wrong-side row.

Wind red and white on bobbins and work rows 1–6 of chart, *right.*

THUMB OPENING: Next row—Work from chart over first 16 (17, 19) sts, work next 5 (6, 6) sts with contrasting color scrap yarn for thumb.

Sl thumb sts back to left needle and k again with red; complete row with red.

Continue to follow chart until chart is completed.

Work even 3 (3, 5) rows, ending with wrong-side row.

TOP SHAPING: *Note*—For position of last stripe, see instructions following top shaping.

Row 1: (K 4, k 2 tog) 5 (5, 6) times, end k 1 (3, 1)—26 (28, 31) sts.

Row 2: Purl.

Row 3: (K 3, k 2 tog) 5 (5, 6) times, end k 1 (3, 1)—21 (23, 25) sts.

Row 4: Purl.

Row 5: (K 2, k 2 tog) 5 (5, 6) times, end k 1 (3, 1)—16 (18, 19) sts.

Row 6: Purl.

Row 7: (K 1, k 2 tog) 5 (5, 6) times, end k 1 (3, 1)—11 (13, 13) sts.

Row 8: Purl.

Row 9: (K 2 tog) 5 (5, 6) times. *Sizes Small and Large:* End k 1. *Size Medium:* End k 1, k 2 tog—6 (7, 7) sts.

Break off and draw tail through rem sts; draw up tightly.

Rep for second mitten, reversing placement of heart motif and thumb opening.

At the same time, work last 1-row (2-row, 2-row) stripe of white beg with Row 2 (Row 5, Row 4) of top shaping.

THUMB: Remove contrast-color scrap yarn; there are 4 (5, 5) lps above opening and 5 (6, 6) lps below opening.

Sl these lps to needles, picking up 2 sts at each side of opening—13 (15, 15) sts. Divide on 3 double-pointed needles.

Rnd 1: Dec 1 st at center of inside of thumb.

Work even 2 rnds—12 (14, 14) sts.

Rep these last 3 rnds twice more—10 (12, 12) sts.

Work even 2 (4, 4) rnds.

K 2 tog around—5 (6, 6) sts.

Break off yarn; draw the tail through the rem sts and draw up tightly.

Sew side seam.

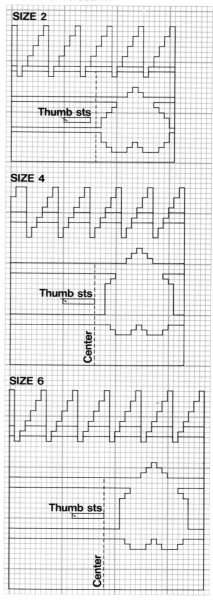

1 Square = 1 Stitch

Granny Glittens and Her Amazing Mittens

—Gertrude Crampton

Once there was an old woman who made mittens from good wool yarn. She made fine warm mittens. Right into the mittens she could knit a boy on a sled, a girl on skates, two yellow ducks, or anything else you could name.

All the mothers and fathers for miles around ordered mittens for their children from Granny Glittens. The needles would flash and knit yarn pictures in the old lady's kitchen from morning till night.

Granny Glittens made mittens because she liked to make mittens. And she made mittens to sell.

Those mittens paid for the coal to keep Granny's little house warm. They paid for the egg for Granny's breakfast. They paid for the milk for Granny's black cat.

Now, of course, Granny Glittens was very busy just before Christmas. Every child wanted a new pair of Granny's mittens for Christmas. Then the needles flashed in the morning and in the evening and in the middle of the day.

But just before Christmas, everything went wrong. Oh, Granny Glittens had orders and orders for mittens. She had so many orders that she kept saying to herself, "Perhaps I can buy a fine new stove for my kitchen."

Yes, the orders came in. It was the yarn that was wrong.

Granny Glittens had to send to the city for yarn. She ordered red yarn and brown yarn and green yarn and yellow yarn and black yarn. But the store sent white yarn—balls and balls of white yarn. Nothing but white yarn!

With the yarn came a letter:

Dear Granny Glittens:
    We do not have red yarn or brown yarn or green yarn or yellow yarn or black yarn. All we have is white yarn.
    We have asked the other stores. They do not have red yarn or brown yarn or green yarn or yellow yarn or black yarn. All they have is white yarn.
    So we are sending you white yarn. We are sorry.

        THE STORE

"Oh, oh, oh!" said Granny Glittens. "Nobody wants white mittens. What shall I do?"

The black cat came into the kitchen. Granny said to him, "I must think. Oh, I must think."

So she thought and thought and thought.

Supper time came. Granny was still thinking. At last the black cat began to cry for milk.

"Poor cat!" she said. "It is dark. You are hungry, and so am I. I will think some more later."

She poured some milk for the cat. Then she opened her cupboard to see what she could find for herself.

Red peppermints, green wintergreen, brown chocolate, black licorice, and yellow lemon drops! They were the colors she needed for her mittens.

"Do you think—" she asked the cat. "Well, the only way to find out is to find out."

She got out five pans from the cupboard. And she put them all on the stove. Then she put the peppermints in one, the wintergreen in another, the chocolate in the third, the licorice in the next, and the lemon drops in the last.

Granny Glittens smiled and smiled. And the next morning the knitting needles flashed and turned.

The new mittens were wonderful. Not ony did they have yellow ducks and fir trees and dancing bears and snow men with black hats. The children could *eat* the yellow ducks and fir trees and dancing bears and snow men with black hats!

Granny Glittens sold so many mittens that she bought a lovely shiny-new stove for her kitchen.

And of course, she was knitting mittens all year round. Because as soon as ever a father or a mother bought a child a pair of mittens the child said they were the best present he ever had—and then ate them! Can you believe it?

Granny Glittens stirred the five pans very carefully with five spoons.

Then she put a ball of white yarn into the peppermints. The yarn turned a beautiful red!

She put a ball of yarn in each pan and stirred more carefully than ever. When each ball was the right color, she took it out and put in another.

It was late that night, and everyone else had been sleeping for hours and hours, before Granny Glittens had all the red and green and brown and yellow and black yarn she needed.

"Oh, my goodness!" she said to the cat. "I am tired. And I am so hungry. I could eat this yarn! I forgot all about my supper."

Just for fun, and to show the cat how hungry she was, Granny Glittens bit off a small piece of red yarn. It tasted good! Granny tasted the other colors too.

Keeping Christmas: GIFTS

Coming up with the right gift for those special people on your Christmas list can seem an overwhelming task, especially if you're a last-minute shopper. We have a solution: four pages of imaginative gift ideas to please family, friends, and others on your list—even beloved pets. Happy holiday shopping!

For Friends

At the same time you buy your Christmas tree, buy a second tree, one that's small. Tie on an assortment of cookie cutters (inexpensive flea market and auction finds) with bright red satin ribbon and deliver the tree to the kitchen of a friend. You're giving a collection she or he will be able to share throughout the holiday season and the rest of the year.

Rummage through boxes of old sheet music you find at flea markets. Frame a copy of *Daddy's Little Girl* for your daughter's room, *I'm a Yankee Doodle Dandy* for someone with a July 4 birthday, or *Oh What a Pal Was Mary!* for a special friend named Mary.

The possibilities are as numerous as the names on your Christmas list.

For Guests

Surprise guests with dessert packages. Tuck a luscious truffle inside a homemade crepe or a purchased one. Tie the bundle with sparkling holiday ribbon.

Treat guests to a take-home delight: a half-dozen sugar cookies neatly stacked between paper doilies and tied in a ribbon.

Tie a ribbon around a small silver spoon engraved with the initial of each guest.

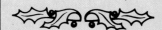

Gifts for Collectors

Browse shops for a pal who collects a specific

item or has a special interest. Call ahead to find out what shopkeepers have on hand and seek out-of-the-way shops.

Buy a collector a good guide book for an antique specialty or a regional history of a collectible.

Sign up a friend for classes in chair caning, refinishing, upholstery, or leaded glass repair.

An antique ring, brooch, or necklace,

wrapped in a small silver box and hidden among the branches of your tree, makes an unexpected surprise for someone special.

Personalize such everyday collectibles as turn-of-the-century kitchen utensils, inexpensive advertising tins, or small items made of silver.

For Crafters
Check antiques shops or vintage clothing stores for old lace trims, buttons, or other interesting notions.

Assemble a pattern, materials, and accessories to make a stuffed

teddy bear. Consider something unusual for the fabric—a piece of old crazy quilt, or woolen plaid, or paisley, for example.

With a sheet of graph paper and some colored pencils or marking pens, create a design for counted cross-stitch. Purchase the fabric, floss, and equipment for the stitchery and present it all in a pretty basket.

Handmade wooden knitting needles and crochet hooks are often for sale at crafts supply shops. Purchase a pair of needles or a crochet hook, along with a couple of skeins of handspun yarn.

Use good areas of badly damaged pieced quilts to make decorative pot holders. Cut the quilt into a square or circle, then

cover the raw edges with purchased bias tape or strips of bias-cut calico. Add a loop for hanging.

For gourmands
Make a poinsettia cake. Use black shoestring licorice to outline a poinsettia on top of a frosted homemade or

bakery cake. Fill the petals and leaves with melted strawberry and mint jelly, then add bits of gumdrops to the center of the flower.

Give gourmet grab bags: a bottle of garlic vinegar, a bottle of sesame oil, one or more jars of unusual

spices (saffron, fines herbes, vanilla beans); specialty coffee beans or teas; a set of kitchen

tools for making garnishes; an herb garden starter set; or a bag of semolina flour for making homemade pasta.

Surprise someone with cookie cutters in traditional shapes and an insulated cookie sheet with a thin layer of air between two aluminum sheets to prevent burning.

For easier cookie making, try a pastry cloth with suction cups that lets you roll out cookies without rolling up the pastry cloth. Dough cutouts easily transfer to baking sheet—no sticking.

Herb vinegar used as a salad dressing is a nice change from plain varieties. To each pint of cider or white vinegar, add any fresh herb—thyme, rosemary, sweet basil, oregano, or dill. Also add a clove of garlic, the peel of a lemon or orange, and six whole

cloves and six dried raisins. Bottle the vinegar in sterilized glass bottles and keep them tightly corked.

Allow the vinegar to mellow three or four weeks before it is used.

Find an antique butter mold and prepare several types of herb butter. Mix fresh cream butter with herbs (such as sweet basil or sage), add chopped parsley or garlic.

Old candy and cookie molds also make great gifts and can double as wall decorations in a country kitchen. Make a batch of cookies or candy with the molds as an extra treat.

For Teens
Surprise your favorite teenager with a gift certificate to an aerobics class or body-shaping club.

Timing is everything: give a plastic fashion watch.

A monogrammed, oversize bath towel will do double duty for showers or beaches.

Grooming supplies are always welcome. Wrap up sunscreen, shampoo, hair conditioner, and lotion from a designer line.

For Nature Lovers
Gather guide books for native flora and fauna, along with a nature diary, and maps and informational materials for state parks, arboretums, or wildlife refuges. (Ask for free information from state and county park or conservation offices.)

Look to mail order seed sources for unusual flowers and herbs. Tie a ribbon around the seed packets and add

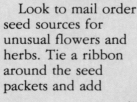

a wish for good planting weather.

Assemble a package of bird seed and a reference book for identifying birds in your area.

For Greetings
Send cards this Christmas that are more than just pretty. UNICEF sells cards to benefit the United Nation's Children's Fund. Sierra Club cards sales help underwrite the organization's environmental programs. Check local chapters of other health, environmental, and social agencies for cards.

For Pets
Reward your faithful companions with mail-order products they can call their own: a dog bed that pampers your pooch with

cotton-soft fiberfill, dinnerware for a finicky feline, or, for the latest in pet gear, a dog-size tent with a sleeping bag.

Wrap up a package of dog biscuits, a glow-

in-the-dark leash, a pet vest or sweater, or a new toy.

Present your favorite feline with a new scratching post.

For Someone Special
At the same time you buy your family Christmas tree, buy a second tree, one that's small. Tie on an assortment of cookie cutters (inexpensive flea market and auction finds) with bright red satin ribbon and deliver the tree to the kitchen of a friend.

It's a collection that he or she will be able to enjoy not only during the holiday season but throughout the coming year as well.

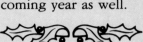

For Kids
Put together a junior tool kit with real hand tools (saw, hammer, clamps).

Scour second-hand stores and antiques shops for a fantasy wardrobe like the items that used to be in Grandma's attic.

Give a child an amusing key chain, complete with a key to the house.

Astonish a child with a magic kit (assemble your own or buy one ready-made.)

Give a practical joker the gift of humor: a joke book and assorted gags from a joke shop.

A birdfeeder, along with birdseed and a book identifying common varieties, will bring hours of pleasure to youngsters.

Children may enjoy an array of toys and games such as those Grandpa and Grandma used to use. Check attics and secondhand stores. Old-fashioned

skates may be decorated and hung on the door of a young sports enthusiast.

Instill an appreciation for finer things right from the start. Purchase single pieces of classic silver for any special occasion. Then, when your child is grown, the set will be complete.

For Wraps
Use plain brown paper as a background for potato stamps, stenciled designs, or adhesive labels.

Travelers will enjoy wraps made of maps from almanacs or the glove compartment.

Choose containers that are both wrapping and little gifts themselves: giant coffee mugs (fill them with special beans), cookie and tobacco tins, reproduction

Shaker cheese and butter boxes, baskets, dinner napkins, a lunch box filled with cookies for your favorite brown-bagger, a simple terra-cotta pot stuffed with seed packets.

Tie on a surprise instead of a bow. Try feathers, seashells, cookie cutters, tiny Christmas tree

ornaments, ar strands of pearls.

Wrap gifts in a swatch of chintz fabric, sheet music, remnant trompe l'oeil wallpaper, and moiré wallpaper finished with chintz roses.

Hand-decorate gift wraps with sponge painting. Begin with a sheet of plain paper and a natural sponge. Dilute the paint to the consistency of light cream and lightly dab the color onto the paper. Work quickly and apply the color randomly.

Work with only one color at a time, but second or third shades can be applied over the original color after the first layer has dried completely.

Spatter-paint papers by dipping a small household brush into paint. Lightly tap the excess from the bristles and spatter the paint onto the paper with a small stick.

To make comb-painted paper, tape a sheet of white or colored glazed paper shiny side up on the work surface. Quickly brush on a layer of acrylic paint (in a color that contrasts with the color of the glazed paper) evenly across the surface of the paper. While the paint

is still wet, create zigzag, swirl, or scallop designs in the paint using a piece of notched cardboard. Let the paint dry.

A Gift for Gramps

—Aileen Fisher

'What are you going to give Gramps for Christmas?' Louella asked her brother as she stared at her Christmas list.

'That's just what I was going to ask you,' replied Johnny. 'I'm stumped.' The two children were sitting alone at the kitchen table. Their half-finished Christmas lists lay before them.

'Gramps always gets socks and handkerchiefs—handkerchiefs and socks,' continued Johnny. 'He has enough to last another hundred years.'

'I know,' said Louella. 'And we can't get him sports things because with his legs so full of rheumatism, poor Gramps just sits in his chair by the window. I wish we could think of something that would be fun for him every day to help him forget his pain.'

So they thought and they thought. Louella closed her eyes, and Johnny stared out of the window at the snowy yard. As he watched, a quick little bird flew to the window-sill, looked into the room, and then flew away.

Suddenly Johnny jumped up from his chair in great excitement. 'I've got it!' he shouted.

'Got what?' asked Louella.

'Why, the present for Gramps. It's perfect, and the whole family could be in on it!'

On Christmas morning, when Gramps had hobbled to his favorite chair by the window, Johnny said, 'Gramps, we wanted to give you something different this year. Something that would be fun for a long time. Now turn around, and look out of the window!'

Gramps turned to look. There, attached to the sill, was a wide new shelf with a molding around its edge. And on the shelf were all sorts of things that birds like to eat: seeds and suet and dabs of peanut butter and bits of dry bread.

'I made the feeding-station,' Johnny explained. 'And Louella got the supply of bird food for you, Gramps.' Johnny held his breath as he saw a snowbird perch on the edge of the feeding-station and then fearlessly peck at some seeds.

'Well, I'll be . . .' Gramps said. 'Look at that!'

Then, with a red and gray flash of wings, another bird swooped down.

'What in the world kind of bird is that?' asked Gramps.

'Ah,' said mother, 'that's where my present comes in.' She reached under the boughs of the Christmas tree and pulled out a package which was hidden there. 'Merry Christmas, Grandpa!'

Gramps opened the package excitedly. There before him was a big book with beautiful colored pictures of hundreds of birds.

'Well, this is something!' Gramps exclaimed, turning the pages. 'I never knew there were so many birds.'

Sometime later, Gramps gave a shout. 'A pine grosbeak! That's what that red and gray bird was: a pine grosbeak!' He grinned with pleasure at being such a good detective. He had forgotten all about his aching rheumatism!

'This is the best Christmas present I ever got,' Gramps said.

Of course, Johnny and Louella received Christmas presents that Christmas too; but what they always remembered best was the gift of giving from their hearts—a gift for Gramps.

Santa Cookie Puppet

If your kids like to spend time in the kitchen, they'll love making this munchable marionette. They can simply copy the Santa character, or use their imaginations to create a cast of colorful Christmas characters.

MATERIALS

For cookie dough
6 cups of flour
1 cup of butter or margarine
2 cups of brown sugar
2 eggs
1 cup of milk
1 teaspoon of vanilla
1 teaspoon of salt
1 teaspoon of baking soda
1 teaspoon of baking powder

For decorating and assembly
Waxed freezer paper
Aluminum foil
Toothpicks
Red, green, white, pink, and chocolate icings
Gumdrops
Four 6-inch-long pipe cleaners for *each* puppet
Six ¼x1x8-inch boards
Colored string
Crafts glue
Frosting decorating bag and tips
Butter knife

INSTRUCTIONS

TO MAKE DOUGH: Cream the butter; add the sugar. Beat until fluffy. Add the vanilla and the eggs; mix. Stir in the milk. Sift together the flour, salt, baking soda, and baking powder. Add to other ingredients; mix until thoroughly blended. Cover; freeze for at least 30 minutes.

While you stir up and chill a large batch of gingerbread dough, trace the puppet pattern, *below* and *opposite,* onto waxed freezer paper. Cut out the pattern pieces.

Place the chilled dough on a sheet of aluminum foil. Roll the dough to ¼-inch thickness.

Arrange the pattern pieces on the rolled-out cookie dough and cut around the shapes with a toothpick (see photo on page 89, *top right*). Poke holes in the body pieces as shown on the patterns. Then, pull away the excess dough around the puppet pieces.

Refrigerate the extra dough, removing 2 cups of dough at a time

for each puppet. (Cold dough is more manageable.) Slide the foil onto a cookie sheet.

Bake in a 400° oven for 10 minutes or until light brown. Let cookies cool before removing.

Cool the puppet pieces, then frost them with icing. Join the puppet pieces with pipe cleaners held in place with gumdrops, as shown on page 89, *bottom right.*

Add the colorful strings and the crossed slats, and the puppets are ready to perform.

TO DECORATE PUPPET: Spread colored frosting onto the cookies with a butter knife for the face and clothing. To trim the cookie fronts, squeeze on icings through decorating tips. Add face and clothing lines. See the photograph on page 88 for color ideas.

TO ASSEMBLE PUPPET: Form a small loop in one end of a 6-inch pipe cleaner. Twist the end around the bottom of the loop to secure it.

Thread the straight end of a pipe cleaner, from the back, through the hole in the shoulder of the arm piece and corresponding shoulder hole in the body.

Position the loop over the hole; pull the straight end up through the loop. Cut off the excess, *leaving at least ½ inch of pipe cleaner for the gumdrop trim.* Push a gumdrop over the end to hold the joint together. Repeat for the remaining three joints.

String the puppets by placing the cookies on a flat surface with puppet arms and legs positioned downward. Using square knots, tie one string to the end of each puppet limb and to the hole in the puppet head.

Cut strings so they all extend 12 inches above the puppet head. For extra strength, place a dab of crafts glue on top of the knots.

Drill a hole ½ inch from the end of each stick and another hole in the middle of each stick. Then, cross the sticks.

Bring the puppet head string through the center stick holes and tie to the upper stick, using a square knot. Bring the arm strings up through the ends of one stick and the leg strings through the other stick. Secure in place with square knots; add crafts glue to the knots. Allow to dry.

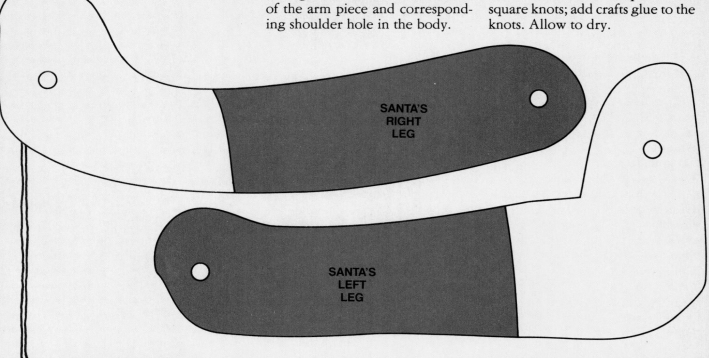

SANTA'S
RIGHT
LEG

SANTA'S
LEFT
LEG

SANTA'S
RIGHT
ARM

SANTA'S
LEFT
ARM

SANTA

The Boy Who Laughed at Santa Claus

In Baltimore there lived a boy.
He wasn't anybody's joy.
Although his name was Jabez Dawes,
His character was full of flaws.
In school he never led the classes,
He hid old ladies' reading glasses,
His mouth was open while he chewed,
And elbows to the table glued.
He stole the milk of hungry kittens,
And walked through doors marked No Admittance.
He said he acted thus because
There wasn't any Santa Claus.
Another trick that tickled Jabez
Was crying "Boo!" at little babies.
He brushed his teeth, they said in town,
Sideways instead of up and down.

Yet people pardoned every sin
And viewed his antics with a grin
Till they were told by Jabez Dawes,
"There isn't any Santa Claus!"
Deploring how he did behave,
His parents swiftly sought their grave.
They hurried through the portals pearly,
And Jabez left the funeral early.
Like whooping cough, from child to child,
He sped to spread the rumor wild:

"Sure as my name is Jabez Dawes
There isn't any Santa Claus!"
Slunk like a weasel or a marten
Through nursery and kindergarten,
Whispering low to every tot,
"There isn't any, no there's not!"
The children wept all Christmas Eve
And Jabez chortled up his sleeve.
No infant dared hang up his stocking
For fear of Jabez' ribald mocking.

continued

He sprawled on his untidy bed,
Fresh malice dancing in his head,
When presently with scalp a-tingling,
Jabez heard a distant jingling;
He heard the crunch of sleigh and hoof
Crisply alighting on the roof.
What good to rise and bar the door?
A shower of soot was on the floor.
What was beheld by Jabez Dawes?
The fireplace full of Santa Claus!
Then Jabez fell upon his knees
With cries of "Don't" and "Pretty please."
He howled, "I don't know where you read it.
But anyhow, I never said it!"

"Jabez," replied the angry saint,
"It isn't I, it's you that ain't.
Although there *is* a Santa Claus,
There isn't any Jabez Dawes!"
Said Jabez then with impudent vim,
"Oh, yes there is; and I am him!
Your magic don't scare me, it doesn't—"
And suddenly he found he wasn't!

From grimy feet to unkempt locks
Jabez became a jack-in-the-box,
An ugly vastly ghastly jack,
In Santa Claus's bulging pack.
The neighbors heard his mournful squeal;
They searched for him, but not with zeal.
No trace was found of Jabez Dawes,
Which led to thunderous applause,
And people drank a loving cup
And went and hung their stockings up.
All you who sneer at Santa Claus,
Beware the fate of Jabez Dawes,
The saucy boy who mocked the saint.
Donner and Blitzen licked off his paint.

—*Ogden Nash*

Gourmet Gifts From Your Kitchen

Remember special friends with a gift from your kitchen this holiday season. Whether your culinary preferences run to sweets, spreads, or snacks, you'll find on the following pages tasty treats to please all of the palates on your gift list. Here are just a few ideas. For a sweet tooth: wrap up a batch of Coconut-Almond Candy Bars or Holiday Chocolate Fans. Tuck a tin of Snappy Cocktail Nuts or Nacho Popcorn in the stocking of a snack-food fan. Surprise a bon vivant with a jar of Roasted Peppers or a container of homemade pasta. For a buddy you break bread with: a Cranberry-Pumpkin Ring or a Mincemeat Bread Wreath.

Pictured clockwise, from lower left, are *Coconut-Almond Candy Bars, Spicy Mulled Beverage Mix, Cocktail Nuts,* and *Caramel Cereal Mix.*

Caramel Cereal Mix

3 cups bite-size shredded
 wheat biscuits
3 cups round toasted oat
 cereal
2 cups pretzel sticks, broken
1½ cups salted peanuts
⅓ cup sugar
¾ cup margarine *or* butter
½ cup light corn syrup
1 teaspoon vanilla

Combine wheat biscuits, oat cereal, pretzels, and peanuts in a large buttered roasting pan. Butter the sides of a 2-quart saucepan. In the pan combine sugar, margarine or butter, and corn syrup. Cook over medium heat to boiling, stirring constantly with a wooden spoon to dissolve sugar.

Cook, stirring frequently, till a candy thermometer registers 280°, soft-crack stage (about 10 minutes). Remove the saucepan from the heat and stir in vanilla. Immediately pour the syrup mixture over the cereal mixture. Stir gently to coat cereal.

Bake in a 350° oven about 20 minutes or till golden brown, stirring once. Transfer cereal mixture onto a large piece of foil. Cool. Break up mixture into small clusters. Store tightly covered. Makes 12 cups.

Fudgy Popcorn

8 cups popped popcorn
⅓ cup margarine *or* butter,
 melted
6 tablespoons instant
 chocolate pudding mix

In a large serving bowl toss the popped popcorn with melted margarine or butter. Sprinkle pudding mix over all and toss with popcorn to coat. Makes 8 cups.

Snappy Cocktail Nuts

3 tablespoons margarine *or*
 butter
2 teaspoons Worcestershire
 sauce
1 teaspoon chili powder *or*
 curry powder
1 teaspoon ground red
 pepper
⅛ teaspoon garlic powder
3 cups cashews or peanuts

In a medium saucepan melt margarine or butter over medium heat. Stir in Worcestershire sauce, chili powder or curry powder, ground red pepper, and garlic powder till well mixed. Add cashews or peanuts, stirring till nuts are evenly coated.

Transfer mixture to a 13x9x2-inch baking pan. Bake nuts in a 300° oven for 20 minutes, stirring twice. Let cool in pan for 15 minutes. Turn out onto paper towels to finish cooling. Makes 3 cups.

Coconut-Almond Candy Bars

3½ cups sifted powdered sugar
1 3-ounce package cream
 cheese, softened
1 teaspoon vanilla
1½ cups coconut
50 blanched whole almonds
 (about ⅓ cup)
1½ pounds chocolate-flavored
 confectioners' coating,
 melted

Butter a 12x9-inch piece of foil; set foil aside. In a small bowl combine powdered sugar, softened cream cheese, and vanilla. Stir in the coconut. Turn the coconut mixture onto the buttered foil. Pat the coconut mixture into a 10x5-inch rectangle. Cut the mixture into 2x1-inch rectangles. Press 2 blanched whole almonds into the top of each rectangle.

Carefully dip the rectangles, one at a time, in the melted coating. Let excess coating drip off rectangles.

Place bars on a baking sheet lined with waxed paper till dry. Store tightly covered in a cool, dry place. Makes 25 candy bars.

Peanut-Caramel Candy Bars

1 14-ounce package vanilla caramels
3 tablespoons margarine *or* butter
2 tablespoons milk
1 cup chopped peanuts
1½ pounds chocolate-flavored confectioners' coating, melted

Line an 8x8x2-inch baking pan with foil, extending the foil over the edges of pan. Butter the foil; set the pan aside.

In a heavy 1½-quart saucepan combine caramels, margarine or butter, and milk. Cook over low heat, stirring occasionally, till caramels are melted. Stir in peanuts. Pour mixture into prepared pan.

Chill about 1 hour or till firm. When firm, use the foil to lift candy out of the pan; cut candy into 2x1-inch rectangles. Carefully dip the rectangles, one at a time, into the melted chocolate coating. Let the excess chocolate drip off the rectangles.

Place bars on a baking sheet lined with waxed paper till dry. Store tightly covered in a cool, dry place. Makes 32 candy bars.

Nacho Popcorn

¼ cup margarine *or* butter, melted
1 teaspoon paprika
½ teaspoon crushed red pepper
½ teaspoon ground cumin
10 cups popped popcorn
⅓ cup grated Parmesan cheese

Combine margarine or butter, paprika, red pepper, and cumin; toss with popcorn. Sprinkle corn with cheese; toss. Makes 10 cups.

Mulled Beverage Mix

1½ cups water
¾ cup sugar
6 inches stick cinnamon, broken
6 whole cloves
   Peel of ¼ lemon, cut into strips
½ cup lemon juice

In a medium saucepan combine water, sugar, cinnamon, cloves, and lemon peel. Bring to boiling; stir till sugar is dissolved. Reduce heat. Simmer, covered, for 10 minutes. Stir in lemon juice. Strain through cheesecloth. Cover tightly; chill in the refrigerator. To serve, in a mug stir 2 tablespoons mix into ¾ cup chilled or heated apple juice or cider, cranberry juice cocktail, dry red or white wine, or rosé wine. Store mix in the refrigerator for up to 6 weeks. Makes 1½ cups mix.

Coffee Crunch Popcorn

8 cups popped popcorn
1 cup peanuts
¾ cup packed brown sugar
⅓ cup butter *or* margarine
3 tablespoons light corn syrup
2 tablespoons instant coffee crystals
¼ teaspoon salt
¼ teaspoon baking soda
¼ teaspoon vanilla

Place popped popcorn and peanuts in a 17x12x2-inch baking pan; set aside. Butter sides of a heavy 1½-quart saucepan. In pan combine brown sugar, margarine or butter, corn syrup, instant coffee crystals, and salt. Bring to boiling. Cook over medium heat for 5 minutes; stir once or twice. Remove from heat. Stir in baking soda and vanilla. Pour over popcorn mixture; stir to coat. Spread evenly in pan. Bake in a 300° oven for 15 minutes; stir. Bake for 5 minutes more. Stir before serving. Makes 10 cups.

Christmas Tree Treats

2 cups all-purpose flour
1 cup whole wheat flour
1 tablespoon baking powder
1 teaspoon ground cinnamon
½ teaspoon ground nutmeg
¼ teaspoon salt
½ cup margarine *or* butter
3 eggs
½ cup milk
2 tablespoons honey
1 12-ounce can date cake and
   pastry filling
½ cup broken walnuts
1 slightly beaten egg white
2 tablespoons honey
   Chopped candied cherries

In a large mixing bowl combine the all-purpose flour, whole wheat flour, baking powder, cinnamon, nutmeg, and salt. Cut in margarine or butter till pieces are the size of small peas. Combine 3 eggs, milk, and 2 tablespoons honey. Add to flour mixture. Stir till combined. On a lightly floured surface, roll out *half* of the dough to ⅛-inch thickness. Use a 4-inch tree cookie cutter to cut 18 trees; reroll dough as necessary. Place on a lightly greased baking sheet. Combine egg white and 2 tablespoons honey. Brush with egg white mixture.

For filling, combine date filling and walnut pieces. Place 1 rounded tablespoon of filling on center of each tree. Roll and cut remaining dough as directed. Place remaining 18 trees over filling. Seal edges with the tines of a fork.

Combine egg white and honey. Brush egg white mixture over each tree. Decorate with cherries. Bake in a 375° oven for 10 to 12 minutes or till light brown. Makes 18 trees.

Cranberry-Pumpkin Ring

1¾ to 2¼ cups unbleached *or*
   all-purpose flour
1 package active dry yeast
½ cup milk
⅓ cup sugar
¼ cup butter *or* margarine
1 teaspoon ground cinnamon
½ teaspoon ground nutmeg
¼ teaspoon ground cloves
1 egg
½ cup canned pumpkin
1¼ cups whole wheat flour
1¼ cups cranberries
⅓ cup sugar
1 teaspoon finely shredded
   orange peel
½ teaspoon ground cinnamon
2 tablespoons butter *or*
   margarine
1 cup sifted powdered sugar
4 teaspoons milk
¼ teaspoon orange extract

In a mixer bowl combine *½ cup* flour and yeast. In a saucepan heat the ½ cup milk, ⅓ cup sugar, ¼ cup butter or margarine, 1 teaspoon cinnamon, nutmeg, cloves, and ¾ teaspoon *salt* till warm (115° to 120°). Add to flour mixture. Beat with an electric mixer on low speed for ½ minute, scraping sides of bowl. Add egg and

pumpkin. Beat for 3 minutes on high speed. Using a spoon, stir in whole wheat flour and as much of the unbleached flour as you can.

Turn out onto floured surface. Knead in enough remaining flour to make a moderately stiff dough that is smooth and elastic (6 to 8 minutes total). Shape into a ball. Place in greased bowl; turn once. Cover; let rise in a warm place till nearly double (about 1 hour).

In a saucepan combine cranberries, ⅓ cup sugar, orange peel, ½ teaspoon cinnamon, and 1 tablespoon *water*. Cook and stir over medium heat till berries pop. Cover and chill in a bowl.

Punch bowl down; let rest for 10 minutes. On a lightly floured surface roll dough into a 15x10-inch rectangle. Spread dough with 2 tablespoons softened butter and then with cranberry filling. Roll up jelly-roll style from long side. Seal seam. Shape into a ring; pinch ends together. Place ring on a greased baking sheet. With kitchen shears, make short cuts from outer edge toward center at 1-inch intervals. Let rise till nearly double (about 30 minutes). Bake ring in a 375° oven for 25 to 30 minutes, covering ring with foil the last 10 minutes to prevent over-browning. Cool on a wire rack.

Combine the powdered sugar, 4 teaspoons milk, and orange extract; drizzle mixture over ring. (Or, omit the glaze. Cool completely; wrap, label, and freeze ring for up to 2 months.) Makes 1 ring, 15 servings.

Mincemeat Bread Wreath

To make the simple apple garnish pictured at right, use hors d'oeuvre cutters to cut two small flower shapes from a slice of apple. Dip in lemon juice to prevent darkening.

1 16-ounce can applesauce
1 9-ounce package instant condensed mincemeat
1 cup apple juice
2 tablespoons margarine *or* butter
1 16-ounce package hot roll mix
1 slightly beaten egg
  Milk (optional)
  Pearl sugar (optional)
  Walnut halves (optional)
  Apple cutouts (optional)
  Lemon leaves (optional)

In a 2-quart saucepan combine applesauce and mincemeat. Bring to boiling; reduce heat. Simmer, uncovered, for 8 to 10 minutes or till thick, stirring occasionally. Cool to room temperature.

Grease a baking sheet; set aside. In a small saucepan heat apple juice and margarine or butter, stirring constantly, till warm (120° to 130°) and margarine or butter is almost melted.

In a large mixing bowl combine flour mixture and yeast from roll mix. Add apple juice mixture and egg. Stir till combined and dough pulls away from sides of bowl. Turn out onto a floured surface; knead for 5 minutes or till smooth. Cover; let rest for 10 minutes.

On a floured surface, roll the dough into a 15x10-inch rectangle. Spread mincemeat mixture on dough to within 1 inch of edges. Roll up from 1 of the long sides; press edges to seal. On prepared baking sheet bring ends together to form a ring; seal ends. With sharp kitchen shears, make 10 vertical cuts at 1½-inch intervals around the outside edge of the ring, cutting to within ½ inch of the inside of the ring. Twist the outside edge of cut pieces to the left, exposing the filling.

Cover; let rise till nearly double (30 to 45 minutes). Brush with a little milk; sprinkle with pearl sugar. Bake in a 350° oven about 30 minutes or till bread sounds hollow when tapped, covering it with foil after 20 minutes of baking to prevent overbrowning. Cool completely on a wire rack.

To freeze, wrap bread in moisture- and vaporproof wrap. Seal, lable, and freeze for up to 6 months. To thaw, let stand, loosely covered, at room temperature for several hours or till thawed.

To serve, top with walnuts. Secure the apple cutouts and lemon leaves to bread with a toothpick. Makes 1 loaf, 12 to 16 servings.

Roasted Peppers

Pictured opposite.

    8 large green peppers
    8 large red, yellow, or purple
       sweet peppers
1½ cups olive *or* cooking oil
 ¾ cup white wine vinegar
    1 tablespoon dried oregano,
       crushed
    1 tablespoon dried basil,
       crushed
 ½ teaspoon salt

Quarter all the peppers length-wise; remove seeds and membrane. Place half at a time, skin side up, in an unheated broiler pan. Broil 3 to 4 inches from the heat about 15 minutes or till charred, turning if necessary to expose all skin surfaces. Place peppers in a paper bag; close tightly. Allow peppers to cool. Peel peppers; place peppers in a bowl.

Combine oil, vinegar, oregano, basil, and salt. Pour the mixture over the peppers; stir gently. Cover; let stand at room temperature about 1 hour, stirring occasionally. Arrange peppers and marinade in 4 decorative 2-cup containers. Store in the refrigerator for up to 4 weeks. Makes 4 (2-cup) gifts.

Marinated Cheese

Pictured opposite.

    1 16-ounce block mozzarella
       cheese
    2 cups olive oil
    1 medium red *or* green sweet
       pepper, cut into strips
 ¼ cup wine vinegar
    1 tablespoon crushed red
       pepper
    1 tablespoon dried oregano,
       crushed
    1 tablespoon green
       peppercorns, crushed
    1 teaspoon dried thyme,
       crushed
    2 cloves garlic, halved

Cut cheese into ½-inch cubes. Randomly prick cubes with a fork. Place cheese in a 1-quart container with a tight-fitting lid. In a small saucepan stir together remaining ingredients. Cook and stir just till heated through. Remove oil mixture from heat; cool. Pour over cheese. Cover; shake gently. Store in the refrigerator about 2 weeks.

Divide the cheese and pepper among 3 decorative 1-cup containers; pour marinade over them to cover. Cover, seal, and label. Store in the refrigerator for 2 weeks before using. Makes 4 (1-cup) gifts.

Carrot Spread

Pictured opposite.

  12 medium carrots, thinly
       sliced (about 2 pounds)
    1 cup sugar
 ½ cup light raisins, chopped
 ¼ cup honey
    3 tablespoons lemon juice
 ¼ cup brandy

In a large saucepan cook the sliced carrots in a small amount of boiling salted water, covered, for 8 to 10 minutes or till very tender; drain. In a blender container or food processor bowl place *one-third* of the cooked carrots. Cover and blend till carrots are pureed; remove. Repeat with the remaining cooked carrots.

In the same saucepan combine all of the carrot puree, the sugar, raisins, honey, and lemon juice. Cook and stir over medium heat for 10 to 15 minutes or till mixture is very thick, stirring frequently. Stir in brandy. Transfer cooked mixture to 4 decorative 1-cup containers or jars. Cover tightly. Store in the refrigerator for up to 1 month. Makes 4 (1-cup) gifts.

Whole-Grain Mustard

1 cup cold water
1 cup dry mustard
¾ cup mustard seed
1¼ cups dry white wine
1 cup vinegar
½ cup packed brown sugar
¼ cup chopped onion
1½ teaspoons ground
  cinnamon
6 whole allspices
½ teaspoon salt
½ teaspoon ground turmeric
2 slightly beaten egg yolks

In a medium mixing bowl stir to-gether the cold water, dry mus-tard, and mustard seed. Let stand about 30 minutes.

In a medium saucepan combine the wine, vinegar, brown sugar, onion, ground cinnamon, all-spices, salt, and turmeric. Bring to boiling; reduce heat. Simmer, un-covered, for 10 to 15 minutes. Strain the vinegar mixture; dis-card the solids.

Stir the egg yolks into the cus-tard mixture. Stir about *1 cup* of the hot liquid into mustard mix-ture. Return all of the mixture to the saucepan. Cook and stir over medium heat till thickened and bubbly. Cook and stir for 2 min-utes more. Remove from heat. Place saucepan in a bowl of ice water; stir for 1 to 2 minutes.

Pour mixture into 5 decorative containers with lids. Store mus-tard in the refrigerator for up to 2 months. Stir before using. Makes 5 (¾-cup) gifts.

Kiwi-and-Pear Preserves

4 kiwi fruits
1 large ripe pear
4 cups sugar
½ of a 6-ounce package
  (1 foil pouch) liquid
  fruit pectin
½ teaspoon finely shredded
  lime or lemon peel
2 tablespoons lime or lemon
  juice

Peel and coarsely chop the kiwi fruit (should measure 1¼ cups). Peel, core, and coarsely chop pear (should measure ¾ cup). In a large bowl mash both fruits with a fork. Stir in sugar. Let stand for 10 minutes. Combine the pectin, lime peel, and lime juice. Add to fruit mixture. Stir for 3 minutes.

Ladle into clean hot jars, leav-ing a ½-inch headspace. Seal and label jars. Let stand overnight till set. Store in therefrigerator for up to 3 weeks. Makes 5 (1-cup) gifts.

Cranberry Sauce

1 pound cranberries (5 cups)
1 12-ounce jar orange
  marmalade
1 cup chopped pecans
1 cup coconut
¾ cup sugar
½ cup water

Combine all of the ingredients. Spread in a 13x9x2-inch baking dish. Bake, uncovered, in a 350° oven about 30 minutes. Transfer to small, attractive jars. Cover and label. Chill. Store in the refrigera-tor. Makes about 4 cups.

Hot Pepper Jelly

1 large green pepper,
  coarsely chopped (1 cup)
2 fresh jalapeño or serrano
  peppers, seeded and
  coarsely chopped
  (⅓ cup)*
6½ cups sugar
1½ cups cider vinegar
½ of a 6-ounce package
  (1 foil pouch) liquid
  fruit pectin
Several drops green food
  coloring

Using the coarse blade of a food grinder, grind green pepper and jalapeño peppers. (Or finely chop green pepper and jalapeño pep-pers using a food processor or knife.) In a 4½-quart Dutch oven combine green pepper mixture, sugar, and vinegar. Bring to boil-ing; reduce heat. Cover; boil gent-ly, stirring frequently, about 15 minutes or till the green pepper mixture becomes transparent. Stir in pectin and food coloring. Re-turn mixture to a full rolling boil; boil hard, uncovered, for 1 min-ute, stirring constantly. Remove from heat. Quickly skim off any foam with a metal spoon. Pour at once into hot sterilized ½-pint jars. Seal, using metal lids or paraf-fin. Store in the refrigerator after opening. Makes 6 half-pints.

*Note: Wear plastic or rubber gloves when chopping hot jala-peño or serrano peppers to avoid contact with volatile oils that can burn skin.

Pesto-Stuffed Pasta

2⅓ cups all-purpose flour
½ teaspoon salt
2 beaten eggs
⅓ cup water
1 teaspoon olive *or* cooking oil
1 cup walnuts
1 cup grated Parmesan cheese (4 ounces)
¼ cup dried parsley flakes
⅛ teaspoon ground red pepper

For basic pasta dough: In a large mixing bowl stir together 2 cups of the flour and the salt. Make a well in the center. In a small mixing bowl combine eggs, water, and oil. Stir egg mixture into the flour mixture all at once, mixing till well combined.

Sprinkle dough with some of the remaining flour. Turn dough out onto a floured surface. Knead till the dough is smooth and elastic (8 to 10 minutes), adding additional flour as needed. Cover; let rest for 10 minutes.

Divide dough into thirds. On a floured surface, roll each third of dough into a 16x12-inch rectangle. If using a pasta machine, pass the dough through the machine till 1/16 inch thick. Dust with additional flour as necessary to prevent sticking. Use the dough to make Pesto-Stuffed Turnovers or Tortellini. Makes about 1 pound.

For pesto filling: In a blender container or food processor bowl combine the walnuts, Parmesan cheese, parsley flakes, and red pepper. Cover and blend the mixture till finely ground, stopping as necessary to push mixture down

the sides of container. Use as filling for the Pesto-Stuffed Turnovers or Tortellini. Makes about 2 cups pasta.

Spinach Pasta: Prepare pasta as directed, *except* combine ¼ cup finely chopped *cooked spinach,* well drained, and ¼ cup *water* with egg and olive oil.

Pesto-Stuffed Turnovers: Using a 1½-inch or 1¾-inch round cutter, cut the dough into circles. Gather up and reroll scraps. Cover cutouts with towel to prevent drying. Place about ¼ teaspoon filling in the center of each circle. To seal in the filling, fold the circle of dough in half to make a half-moon. Moisten the edge of dough with water; press edges together with fingers. Arrange turnovers in a single layer on floured surface; let stand overnight. Divide the pasta among 3 airtight containers. Makes 3 (6-ounce) gifts.

Pesto-Stuffed Tortellini: Prepare the half-moons as for pasta turnovers. Place your index finger against the fold; bend turnover around your finger, bringing the outer corners together. Press one corner over the other, moistening if necessary. Pinch the ends firmly together to secure the tortellini. Arrange the shaped pasta in a single layer on floured surface; let stand overnight. For giving, divide the tortellini among 3 airtight containers.

Serve this pasta as a side dish with your favorite cream sauce or tomato sauce. Store in a dry place at room temperature for up to 2 months. To cook, bring 2 quarts water to a rolling boil. Add oil to help keep pasta separated. When water boils, add the pasta a little at a time so the water does not stop boiling. Reduce the heat and continue boiling gently, uncovered, till the pasta is tender (about 3 to 4 minutes). Drain.

Carrot Marmalade

6 medium carrots, shredded
2 medium tart cooking apples, peeled, cored, and finely chopped
1 medium pear, peeled, cored, and finely chopped
2 cups sugar
1 cup honey
2 teaspoons finely shredded lime peel
⅓ cup lime juice

In a 4-quart Dutch oven combine carrots, apples, pear, sugar, honey, lime peel, and lime juice. Bring to boiling; reduce heat. Boil gently, uncovered, for 35 to 40 minutes or till thickened, stirring often. Ladle marmalade into hot, clean ½-pint jars, leaving a ¼-inch headspace. Wipe jar rims; adjust lids. Process in boiling-water bath for 15 minutes (start timing when water boils). Store in the refrigerator after opening for up to 6 months. Makes 4 to 5 half-pints.

Mocha Nut Divinity

2½ cups sugar
½ cup light corn syrup
¼ cup instant Swiss-style
    coffee powder
2 egg whites
1 cup chopped pecans

In a saucepan combine the sugar, corn syrup, coffee powder, and ½ cup *water*. Cook over medium-high heat to boiling, stirring constantly to dissolve sugar, 5 to 7 minutes. Cook over medium heat, without stirring, till the thermometer registers 260° (about 15 minutes). Remove from heat.

In a large mixer bowl immediately beat the egg whites with a standard-size electric mixer on medium speed till stiff peaks form (tips stand straight). Gradually pour hot mixture in a thin stream over egg whites, beating on high speed and scraping the sides of the bowl occasionally, about 3 minutes. Continue beating on high speed till candy starts to lose its gloss, about 6 to 7 minutes. Fold in the nuts. Quickly drop candy onto a baking sheet lined with waxed paper. Makes about 40 pieces (1¼ pounds).

Red Raspberry Truffles

½ cup *sweetened condensed*
    milk
½ cup light cream
5 ounces semisweet
    chocolate, melted
4 ounces unsweetened
    chocolate, melted
2 egg yolks
2 tablespoons amaretto
2 tablespoons raspberry
    liqueur
    Fresh *or* frozen raspberries
    Cocoa powder (optional)
    Coconut (optional)
    Finely chopped nuts
    (optional)
    Powdered sugar (optional)

In a medium heavy saucepan combine condensed milk and light cream; bring just to boiling. Remove from heat and cool for 5 minutes. In a food processor bowl with a steel blade, combine milk mixture and chocolate; process for 5 to 10 seconds. Add egg yolks; process for 5 seconds. Add liqueurs; process for 5 seconds.

Pour mixture into a large mixing bowl; place bowl in a larger container with ice packed around bowl. *Be sure no water or ice gets into the mixture.* Stir till thick and completely cool. Immediately whip with an electric mixer about 2 minutes or till soft peaks form. Cool till firm (about 1 hour).

Using 1 tablespoon of mixture for each, shape into balls, filling each with a whole raspberry. Roll in cocoa powder, coconut, finely chopped nuts, or powdered sugar. Store in a cool, dry place for 7 to 10 days. Makes about 36.

Carob-Peanut Clusters

Pictured opposite.

1 cup quick-cooking rolled
    oats
1 cup sugar
3 tablespoons carob powder
⅓ cup evaporated milk
¼ cup butter *or* margarine
¼ cup peanut butter
½ cup peanuts

To toast oats: place oats in a layer in a 15x10x1-inch baking pan. Bake in a 350° oven for 15 to 20 minutes, stirring occasionally.

In a saucepan combine sugar and carob powder; add milk and butter or margarine. Bring to a full rolling boil over medium heat. Boil gently for 1 minute, stirring constantly. Remove from heat. Stir in peanut butter. Pour over oats and peanuts in a bowl; stir to combine. Let cool slightly. Drop by teaspoons onto waxed paper. Chill. Makes 36 pieces.

Nutcracker Suite Tart

Pictured above.

3⅓ cups all-purpose flour
¼ cup sugar
1 cup butter *or* margarine
2 slightly beaten egg yolks
1 cup sugar
⅓ cup honey
3½ cups chopped pistachio
    nuts (about 1 pound)
1 cup milk
¼ cup butter *or* margarine
⅓ cup seedless raspberry jam
2 tablespoons crème de cassis
¼ cup finely chopped
    pistachio nuts (about
    1 ounce)

Stir together flour and the ¼ cup sugar; cut in the 1 cup butter or margarine till pieces are the size of small peas. Add egg yolks and ⅓ cup *water;* toss with a fork till moistened. Form into a ball; wrap and chill. In a saucepan combine 1 cup sugar, honey, and ½ cup *water.* Bring to boiling, stirring till sugar is dissolved. Reduce heat to low; boil gently for 25 minutes or till caramel colored. Stir in 3½ cups nuts, milk, and ¼ cup butter. Return to boiling; boil over low heat for 15 minutes more. On a lightly floured surface roll *one-fourth* of the chilled dough into an 11-inch circle; fit into a 9-inch flan pan, quiche dish, or cake pan; pour *half* of the nut mixture into the crust.

Roll out another *one-fourth* of the dough into an 11-inch circle; cut slits. Place over filling. Trim top crust ½ inch beyond edge of pan. Fold extra pastry over top crust; flute edges, sealing well. Repeat for second tart. Bake in a 425° oven for 30 to 35 minutes. Cool. Invert onto a serving platter. In a saucepan, combine jam and crème de cassis; heat till jam is melted. Spoon over tart. Garnish with remaining nuts. Chill. (Or, wrap the tart in moisture- and vaporproof wrap. Seal, label, and freeze. To serve, thaw, then spoon melted jam over tart.) Makes 2 tarts, 8 to 12 servings each.

Holiday Chocolate Fans

1 1-pound package frozen phyllo dough
1 cup butter *or* margarine, melted
1 12-ounce package semisweet chocolate pieces
2 teaspoons finely shredded orange peel
2 tablespoons shortening
1 teaspoon ground cinnamon
½ teaspoon ground nutmeg
1 cup coconut *or* finely chopped pistachios, pecans, *or* walnuts

Thaw the phyllo dough according to package directions. Cut rolled phyllo dough in paper wrapper crosswise into fifths. Rewrap 4 of the pieces in damp towels. Unroll 1 fifth of the phyllo, discarding paper. Cut strip in half crosswise. Take 1 phyllo sheet layer; brush with melted butter. Repeat with a third sheet. Fold sheets into ¾-inch folds, starting at a short end and forming an accordion. Pinch together the folds at 1 end; spread folds apart at the other end, forming a fan shape.

Place on an ungreased baking sheet. Repeat with remainder of first fifth of phyllo. Bake 6 fans at a time in a 375° oven about 5 minutes or till golden brown. Transfer to a wire rack; cool. Repeat with remaining phyllo, one at a time, keeping each wrapped till used.

Melt chocolate over low heat; stir in orange peel, shortening, cinnamon, and nutmeg. Dip the wide end of each fan in chocolate (about ¼ inch); then dip in coconut or nuts. Place on a rack to harden chocolate. Makes 65 fans.

Santa's Elves' Holiday Treats

Pictured above.

2 cups vanilla wafer crumbs
½ cup melted butter *or* margarine
2 cups sifted powdered sugar
1 8-ounce package cream cheese, softened
1 cup butter *or* margarine, softened
2 eggs
4 medium bananas
1 cup coconut
1 8-ounce carton frozen whipped dessert topping, thawed
1 cup chopped walnuts
Small candy canes (optional)
Banana slices (optional)

Combine the crumbs and melted butter; press into the bottom of a 13x9x2-inch pan. Beat powdered sugar, cream cheese, and the 1 cup butter or margarine till smooth. Add eggs; beat till fluffy. Spread over crust. Arrange the bananas over top; sprinkle with coconut. Spread dessert topping over all; sprinkle with nuts. Cover; chill for several hours. Cut into squares. Garnish each serving with a candy cane and banana slices, if desired. Makes 12 servings.

Home for
The Holidays

A Tree to Remember

At least once each year while making Christmas cookies, I glance into the living room to make sure the tree still stands. It's the cookies that remind me of the year that the tree, fully loaded with cookie ornaments, toppled over—helped on its way by the family dog. The dog only wanted a bite of one glittering pig, a cookie ornament studded with dozens of tiny silver candies as hard as jawbreakers. The silver BBs ran in tiny crooked rows on top of the pig's fuchsia frosting. After the tree had gone down, the only sound in the room was the dog crunching on those little silver shots.

The children were 4 and 6 that year; in those halcyon days they wanted to help with everything or, better yet, do it themselves. "I do it, I do it myself!" was like a war cry in our house. We had baked bread together—why not bake our own ornaments? So we left in boxes my grandmother's blown-glass bugles and Santas.

I found a recipe for salt dough for the ornaments. Then I considered how all three of us liked to eat raw cookie dough (a forbidden delicacy in my own childhood) and how the children would eat the salt dough and get sick. We made batches of sugar cookie dough instead, adding extra flour and egg to make the dough denser.

I had a collection of old cookie cutters. Some were the vintage of Grandmother's glass ornaments— lions and pigs and birds, dogs and stars and angels. We used them and our dough to make cookies that were as thick and heavy as proverbial lead. The children layered on frosting in lurid colors. Before the frosting hardened, they pressed in sprinkles and the little silver candies.

When the cookies were done, the children wanted to make icicles for the tree. So I went out for carrots, picking the smallest, skinniest ones I could find. We made more frosting, but added white school glue to it in liberal doses. The children smeared this plaster on the carrots, then rolled their icicles in silver glitter. We managed to push a wire through each icicle to hang it.

Luckily, the tree we'd cut that year had sturdy branches. Even so, the weight of our ornaments bowed them down—the finished look was rather startling. Of course, the children could only see its beauty.

On Christmas Eve my husband took snapshots of the children standing at either side of their masterpiece. Lucky to have film in the camera for once, as we'd not long to enjoy their work. It was after he'd put away the camera, when the children were hanging their stockings, that the dog did her work.

I saw the dog eyeing the tree. I saw her put up a paw in a tentative, catlike way. But I'd momentarily turned my back when she chanced her amazing lunge. I turned in time to see the tree heading toward the fireplace, the children leaping out of its path.

Our cookie ornaments shattered as they hit the floor. The icicles were only carrots again; their glitter lay about us in small broken bits.

Amid the children's tears, we righted the tree, screwing it even more tightly into its stand. The dog knew her disgrace. She squeezed herself underneath the couch and could not be coaxed out. In her single-mindedness, however, she'd taken with her the silver pig.

After we'd put the children to bed, I spent some time rearranging the ornaments we had left. Then, giving up, I pulled out Grandmother's glass baubles. As I began slipping them on the empty branches, something inside me said, "stop." Instead, I draped on another string of lights and walked across the room to have a look.

I could hear the dog lapping water in the kitchen. After a few moments she came and lay down at my feet. Poor old thing, she'd been scolded enough. All that glitter and flash had been too much for her to resist. It was Christmas, after all. I went to the refrigerator and found the marrow bone we'd tied up in a red bow. She took it under the tree and began to chew, in dog ecstasy.

I stood in the kitchen doorway. It was nearly midnight. The tree cast silver and red light through the bay window and out into the snowy night. The carrot icicles turned to ruddy gold. Silver ponies and dogs with their sprinkle trappings moved slowly in the rush of air from the floor register. We'd done such loving work and preserved at least one photograph of it for posterity. Surely, this would be the Christmas tree we'd never forget.

—By Pauline W. Wanderer

Christmas Under the Snow

—Olive Thorne Miller

It was just before Christmas, and Mr. Barnes was starting for the nearest village. The family were out at the door to see him start, and give him the last charges.

"Don't forget the Christmas dinner, papa," said Willie.

" 'Specially the chickens for the pie!" put in Nora.

"An' the waisins," piped up little Tot, standing on tiptoe to give papa a good-bye kiss.

"I hate to have you go, George," said Mrs. Barnes anxiously. "It looks to me like a storm."

"Oh, I guess it won't be much," said Mr. Barnes lightly; "and the youngsters must have their Christmas dinner, you know."

"Well," said Mrs. Barnes, "remember this, George: if there is a bad storm don't try to come back. Stay in the village till it is over. We can get along alone for a few days, can't we, Willie?" turning to the boy who was giving the last touches to the harness of old Tim, the horse.

"Oh, yes! Papa, I can take care of mamma," said Willie earnestly.

"And get up the Christmas dinner out of nothing?" asked papa, smiling.

"I don't know," said Willie, hesitating, as he remembered the proposed dinner, in which he felt a deep interest.

"What could you do for the chicken pie?" went on papa with a roguish look in his eye, "or the plum-pudding?"

"Or the waisins?" broke in Tot anxiously.

"Tot has set her heart on the raisins," said papa, tossing the small maiden up higher than his head, and dropping her all laughing on the door-step, "and Tot shall have them sure, if papa can find them in S—. Now good-bye, all! Willie, remember to take care of mamma, and I depend on you to get up a Christmas dinner if I don't get back. Now, wife, don't worry!" were his last words as the faithful old horse started down the road.

Mrs. Barnes turned one more glance to the west, where a low, heavy bank of clouds was slowly rising, and went into the little house to attend to her morning duties.

"Willie," she said, when they were all in the snug little log-cabin in which they lived, "I'm sure there's going to be a storm, and it may be snow. You had better prepare enough wood for two or three days; Nora will help bring it in."

"Me, too!" said grave little Tot.

"Yes, Tot may help too," said mamma.

This simple little home was a busy place, and soon every one was hard at work. It was late in the afternoon before the pile of wood, which had been steadily growing all day, was high enough to satisfy Willie, for now there was no doubt about the coming storm, and it would probably bring snow; no one could guess how much, in that country of heavy storms.

"I wish the village was not so far off, so that papa could get back to-night," said Willie, as he came in with his last load.

Mrs. Barnes glanced out of the window. Broad scattering snowflakes were silently falling; the advance guard, she felt them to be, of a numerous host.

"So do I," she replied anxiously, "or that he did not have to come over that dreadful prairie, where it is so easy to get lost."

"But old Tim knows the way, even in the dark," said Willie proudly. "I believe Tim knows more'n some folks."

"No doubt he does, about the way home," said mamma, "and we won't worry about papa, but have our supper and go to bed. That'll make the time seem short."

The meal was soon eaten and cleared away, the fire carefully covered up on the hearth, and the whole little family quietly in bed. Then the storm, which had been making ready all day, came down upon them in earnest. The bleak wind howled around the corners, the white flakes by millions and millions came with it, and hurled themselves upon that house. In fact, that poor little cabin alone on the wide prairie seemed to be the object of their sport. They sifted through the cracks in the walls, around the windows, and under the door, and made pretty little drifts on the floor. They piled up against it outside, covered the steps, and then the door, and then the windows, and then the roof, and at last buried it completely out of sight under the soft, white mass.

And all the time the mother and her three children lay snugly covered up in their beds fast asleep, and knew nothing about it.

The night passed away and morning came, but no light broke through the windows of the cabin. Mrs. Barnes woke at the usual time, but finding it still dark and perfectly quiet outside, she concluded that the storm was over, and with a sigh of relief turned over to sleep again. About eight o'clock, however, she could sleep no more, and became wide awake enough to think the darkness strange. At that moment the clock struck, and the truth flashed over her.

Being buried under snow is no uncommon thing on the wide prairies, and since they had wood and cornmeal in plenty, she would not have been much alarmed if her husband had been home. But snow deep enough to bury them must cover up all landmarks, and she knew her husband would not rest till he had found them. To get lost on the trackless prairie was fearfully easy, and to suffer and die almost in sight of home was no unusual thing, and was her one dread in living there.

A few moments she lay quiet in bed, to calm herself and get control of her own anxieties before she spoke to the children.

"Willie," she said at last, "are you awake?"

"Yes, mamma," said Willie; "I've been awake ever so long; isn't it almost morning?"

"Willie," said the mother quietly, "we mustn't be frightened, but I think—I'm afraid—we are snowed in."

Willie bounded to his feet and ran to the door.

"Don't open it!" said mamma hastily; "the snow may fall in. Light a candle and look out the window."

In a moment the flickering rays of the candle fell upon the window. Willie drew back the curtain. Snow was tightly banked up against it to the top.

"Why, mamma," he explained, "so we are! and how can papa find us? and what shall we do?"

"We must do the best we can," said mamma, in a voice which she tried to make steady, "and trust that it isn't very deep, and that Tim and papa will find us, and dig us out."

By this time the little girls were awake and inclined to be very much frightened, but mamma was calm now, and Willie was brave and hopeful.

They all dressed, and Willie started the fire. The smoke refused to rise, but puffed out into the room, and Mrs. Barnes knew that if the chimney were closed they would probably suffocate, if they did not starve or freeze.

The smoke in a few minutes choked them, and, seeing that something must be done, she put the two girls, well wrapped in blankets, into the shed outside the back door, closed the door to keep out the smoke, and then went with Willie to the low attic, where a scuttle door opened onto the roof.

"We must try," she said, "to get it open without letting in too much snow, and see if we can manage to clear the chimney."

"I can reach the chimney from the scuttle with a shovel," said Willie. "I often have with a stick."

continued

After much labour, and several small avalanches of snow, the scuttle was opened far enough for Willie to stand on the top round of the short ladder, and beat a hole through to the light, which was only a foot above. He then shovelled off the top of the chimney, which was ornamented with a big round cushion of snow, and then by beating and shovelling he was able to clear the door, which he opened wide, and Mrs. Barnes came up on the ladder to look out. Dreary indeed was the scene! Nothing but snow as far as the eye could reach, and flakes still falling, though lightly. The storm was evidently almost over, but the sky was gray and overcast.

They closed the door, went down, and soon had a fire, hoping that the smoke would guide somebody to them.

Breakfast was taken by candle-light, dinner—in time—in the same way, and supper passed with no sound from the outside world.

Many times Willie and mamma went to the scuttle door to see if any one was in sight, but not a shadow broke the broad expanse of white over which toward night the sun shone. Of course there were no signs of the roads, for through so deep snow none could be broken, and until the sun and frost should form a crust on top there was little hope of their being reached.

The second morning broke, and Willie hurried up to his post of lookout first thing. No person was in sight, but he found a light crust on the snow, and the first thing he noticed was a few half-starved birds trying in vain to pick up something to eat. They looked weak and almost exhausted, and a thought struck Willie.

It was hard to keep up the courage of the little household. Nora had openly lamented that to-night was Christmas Eve, and no Christmas dinner to be had. Tot had grown very tearful about her "waisins," and Mrs. Barnes, though she tried to keep up heart, had become very pale and silent.

continued

Willie, though he felt unbounded faith in papa, and especially in Tim, found it hard to suppress his own complaints when he remembered that Christmas would probably be passed in the same dismal way, with fears for papa added to their own misery.

The wood, too, was getting low, and mamma dared not let the fire go out, as that was the only sign of their existence to anybody; and though she did not speak of it, Willie knew, too, that they had not many candles, and in two days at farthest they would be left in the dark.

The thought that struck Willie pleased him greatly, and he was sure it would cheer up the rest. He made his plans, and went to work to carry them out without saying anything about it.

He brought out of a corner of the attic an old box-trap he had used in the summer to catch birds and small animals, set it carefully on the snow, and scattered crumbs of corn-bread to attract the birds.

In half an hour he went up again, and found to his delight he had caught bigger game—a poor rabbit which had come from no one knows where over the crust to find food.

This gave Willie a new idea; they could save their Christmas dinner after all; rabbits made very nice pies. Poor Bunny was quietly laid to rest, and the trap set again. This time another rabbit was caught, perhaps the mate of the first. This was the last of the rabbits, but the next catch was a couple of snowbirds. These Willie carefully placed in a corner of the attic, using the trap for a cage, and giving them plenty of food and water.

When the girls were fast asleep, with tears on their cheeks for the dreadful Christmas they were going to have, Willie told mamma about his plans. Mamma was pale and weak with anxiety, and his news first made her laugh and then cry. But after a few moments given to her long pent-up tears, she felt much better and entered into his plans heartily.

The two captives up in the attic were to be Christmas presents for the girls, and the rabbits were to make the long anticipated pie. As for plum-pudding, of course that couldn't be thought of.

"But don't you think, mamma," said Willie eagerly, "that you could make some sort of a cake out of meal, and wouldn't hickory nuts be good in it? You know I have some left up in the attic, and I might crack them softly up there, and don't you think they would be good?" he concluded anxiously.

"Well, perhaps so," said mamma, anxious to please him and help him in his generous plans. "I can try. If I only had some eggs—but seems to me I have heard that snow beaten into cake would make it light—and there's snow enough, I'm sure," she added with a faint smile, the first Willie had seen for three days.

The smile alone he felt to be a great achievement, and he crept carefully up the ladder, cracked the nuts to the last one, brought them down, and mamma picked the meats out, while he dressed the two rabbits which had come so opportunely to be their Christmas dinner.

"Wish you Merry Christmas!" he called out to Nora and Tot when they waked. "See what Santa Claus has brought you!"

Before they had time to remember what a sorry Christmas it was to be, they received their presents, a live bird, for each, a bird that was never to be kept in a cage, but fly about the house till summer came, and then go away if it wished.

Pets were scarce on the prairie, and the girls were delighted. Nothing papa could have brought them would have given them so much happiness.

They thought no more of the dinner, but hurried to dress themselves and feed the birds, which were quite tame from hunger and weariness. But after a while they saw preparations for dinner, too. Mamma made a crust and lined a deep dish—the chicken pie dish—and then she brought a mysterious something out of the cupboard, all cut up so that it looked as if it might be chicken, and put it in the dish with other things, and then she tucked them all under a thick crust, and set it down in a tin oven before the fire to bake. And that was not all. She got out some more cornmeal, and made a batter, and put in some sugar and something else which she slipped in from a bowl, and which looked in the batter something like raisins; and at the last moment Willie brought her a cup of snow and she hastily beat it into the cake, or pudding, whichever you might call it, while the children laughed at the idea of making a cake out of snow. This went into the same oven and pretty soon it rose up light and showed a beautiful brown crust, while the pie was steaming through little fork holes on top, and sending out most delicious odors.

At the last minute, when the table was set and everything ready to come up, Willie ran up to look out of the scuttle, as he had every hour of daylight since they were buried. In a moment came a wild shout down the ladder.

"They're coming! Hurrah for old Tim!"

Mamma rushed up and looked out, and saw—to be sure—old Tim slowly coming along over the crust, drawing after him a wood sled on which were two men.

"It's papa!" shouted Willie, waving his arms to attract their attention.

"Willie!" came back over the snow in tones of agony. "Is that you? Are all well?"

"All well!" shouted Willie, "and just going to have our Christmas dinner."

"Dinner?" echoed papa, who was now nearer. "Where is the house, then?"

"Oh, down here!" said Willie, "under the snow, but we're all right, only we mustn't let the plum-pudding spoil."

Looking into the attic, Willie found that mamma had fainted away, and this news brought to her aid papa and the other man, who proved to be a good friend who had come to help.

Tim was tied to the chimney, whose thread of smoke had guided them home, and all went down into the dark room. Mrs. Barnes soon recovered, and while Willie dished up the smoking dinner, stories were told on both sides.

Mr. Barnes had been trying to get through the snow and to find them all the time, but until the last night had made a stiff crust he had been unable to do so.

Then Mrs. Barnes told her story, winding up with the account of Willie's Christmas dinner. "And if it hadn't been for his keeping up our hearts I don't know what would have become of us," she said at last.

"Well, my son," said papa, "you did take care of mamma, and get up a dinner out of nothing, sure enough; and now we'll eat the dinner, which I am sure is delicious."

So it proved to be; even the cake, or pudding, which Tot christened snow pudding, was voted very nice, and the hickory nuts as good as raisins.

When they had finished, Mr. Barnes brought in his packages, gave Tot and the rest some "sure-enough waisins," and added his Christmas presents to Willie's; but though all were overjoyed, nothing was quite so nice in their eyes as the two live birds.

After dinner the two men and Willie dug out passages from the doors, through the snow, which had wasted a good deal, uncovered the windows, and made a slanting way to his shed for old Tim. Then for two or three days Willie made tunnels and little rooms under the snow, and for two weeks, while the snow lasted, Nora and Tot had fine times in the little snow playhouses.

Tiny Treasures For the Tree

One of the most enduring symbols of the Christmas season is the tree, bedecked in all its finery. To add your own personal stamp to this year's evergreen, craft one or more of the ornaments you'll find here and on the pages that follow. They include elegant crocheted hearts, aromatic cinnamon shapes, painted wooden figures, fabric hearts, and folksy paper trims.

Openwork Crocheted Heart Ornaments

Finished size is about 4½ inches across heart at widest point.

MATERIALS
1 ball of DMC Cébélia
 crochet cotton, Size 10
Size 6 steel crochet hook

Gauge: In rows of dc, 9 dc = 1 inch.

INSTRUCTIONS
Ch 8, sl st to form ring.
Rnd 1: Ch 5, dc in ring, (ch 3, trc in ring) 7 times, ch 3, dc in ring, ch 2, sl st in third st of beginning ch-5.

Rnd 2: Ch 3, dc in next dc, make (ch 3 and trc) 5 times in first trc, trc in next trc, ch 2, trc in next trc, make (ch 3 and trc) 4 times in next trc, ch 3, trc in next trc, ch 2, trc in next trc, make (trc and ch 3) 5 times in last trc, dc in last dc, ch 3, sl st at the start of the row.

Rnd 3: Make 3 sc over ch-3, sc in dc, 3 hdc over next ch-3, (dc in next trc, 5 dc over ch-3) 3 times, dc in next trc, 3 dc over ch-3, dc in trc, hdc in next trc, 2 sc over ch-2, (sc in trc, 3 sc over ch-3) twice, hdc in trc, 5 dc over ch-3 at tip of heart. Now, continue up the other side: Hdc in trc, (3 sc over ch-3, sc in trc) twice, 2 sc over ch-2, hdc in trc, dc in next trc, 3 dc over ch-3, (dc in trc, 5 dc over ch-3) 3 times, dc in trc, 3 hdc over ch-3, sc in dc, 3 sc over last ch-3, sl st in first sc made.

Rnd 4: Sl st in second, third, and fourth sc, ch 7, sk 3 hdc, trc in first dc, (ch 5, sk 2 dc, trc in next dc) 6 times, (ch 5, sk 3 sts, trc in next st) 4 times, ch 5, make (trc, ch 5, trc) in center dc of point, ch 5, sk 2 dc, trc in hdc, (ch 5, sk 3 sts, trc in next st) 4 times, (ch 5, sk 2 dc, trc in next dc) 6 times, ch 3, sk 3 hdc, trc in sc, sl st in fourth st of first ch-7.

Rnd 5: Make 3 sc over ch-3 sp, then work in each ch-5 sp as follows: Make (3 dc, ch 3, sl st in top of last dc just made for picot, 3 dc in same sp) all around, then make 3 sc in the last ch-3 sp. Sl st in the first sc made and fasten off.

Filet-Crocheted Heart Ornaments

Finished size is about 4½ inches across heart at widest point.

MATERIALS
1 ball of DMC Cébélia
   crochet cotton, Size 10
Size 6 steel crochet hook

Gauge: 9 dc = 1 inch.

INSTRUCTIONS
FIRST SECTION: Row 1—Ch 4, make 4 dc in fourth ch from hook. Ch 3, turn.

Row 2: Make 2 dc in first dc, ch 1, sk 1 dc, dc in next dc, ch 1, sk 1 dc, 3 dc in top of turning ch. Ch 3, turn.

Row 3: Make 2 dc in first dc, ch 1, sk 1 dc, dc in next dc, (dc in ch-1 sp, dc in next dc) twice, ch 1, sk 1 dc, 3 dc in top of turning ch. Ch 3, turn.

Rows 4–7: Work 2 dc in first dc, ch 1, sk 1 dc, dc in next dc, dc in ch-1 sp, dc in each dc across center section, dc in ch-1 sp, dc in next dc, ch 1, sk 1 dc, 3 dc in top of turning ch. Ch 3, turn. There will be 21 dc in center section on Row 7.

Row 8: Sk first dc, dc in next 2 dc, ch 1, dc in each of 21 dc, ch 1, dc in last 2 dc and in top of turning ch. Ch 3, turn.

Row 9: Sk first dc, dc in next 2 dc, ch 1, dc in next 9 dc, (ch 1, sk 1 dc, dc in next dc) twice, dc in remaining 8 dc of center, ch 1, dc in last 2 dc and in top of turning ch. Turn.

Row 10: Sl st in second dc, ch 3, dc in next dc and in ch-1 sp, ch 1, sk 1 dc, dc in each of next 6 dc, ch 1. Holding back on hook last lp of each st, make dc in last dc and in ch-1 sp, yarn over and pull through all lps on hook—2-dc cluster made. Turn.

Row 11: Ch 3, dc in ch-1 sp, (dc in next dc, ch 1, sk next dc) 3 times, dc in ch-1 sp and in next 2 dc. Turn.

Row 12: Sl st in second dc, ch 3, (dc in next dc and in ch-1 sp) 3 times, dc in next 2 dc, ch 3, sl st in top of turning ch. Make sl st in side of same turning ch. Make sl st in side of same turning ch and in top of cluster on Row 10, ch 3 and sl st in center dc of Row 9, then make second section of heart as follows.

SECOND SECTION: Row 10—Ch 3, make a 2-dc cluster in ch-1 sp and first dc, ch 1, sk 1 dc, dc in each of next 6 dc, ch 1, sk last dc, dc in ch-1 sp and next 2 dc. Turn.

Row 11: Sl st in second dc, ch 3, dc in next dc and in ch-1 sp, (ch 1, sk 1 dc, dc in next dc) 3 times, dc in ch-1 sp and in cluster st. Ch 3, turn.

Row 12: Sk first dc, dc in next 2 dc, (dc in ch-1 sp, dc in next dc) 3 times, dc in next dc. There will be a total of 9 dc plus the turning ch on this row. Now continue down side of heart to make edging.

EDGING: Rnd. 1—(Ch 5, sc in top corner of previous row) 11 times, ch 5, dc in point of heart, (ch 5, sc in top corner of next row) 12 times, (ch 5, sk 2 dc, sc in next

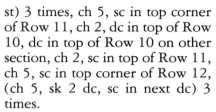

st) 3 times, ch 5, sc in top corner of Row 11, ch 2, dc in top of Row 10, dc in top of Row 10 on other section, ch 2, sc in top of Row 11, ch 5, sc in top corner of Row 12, (ch 5, sk 2 dc, sc in next dc) 3 times.

Rnd 2: Sl st to center of next ch-5 lp. (Ch 5, sc in next lp) 11 times around to point, ch 5, make (dc, ch 5, dc) in dc at point, (ch 5, sc in next lp) 16 times, ch 2, dc bet the 2 dc at center, ch 2 (sc in next ch-5 lp, ch 5) 4 times, sl st to start of rnd.

Rnd 3: Make (sc, hdc, dc, ch 3, sl st in top of dc just made for picot, hdc, sc) in each ch-5 lp around. At top of heart make 2 sc in each of the ch-2 sps. After last scallop is completed, join with sl st in first sc on rnd and fasten off.

Small Crocheted Heart Ornaments

Finished size is about 2½ inches across heart at widest point.

MATERIALS
1 ball of DMC Cébélia
   crochet cotton, Size 10
Size 6 steel crochet hook

Gauge: In rows of dc, 9 dc = 1 inch.

INSTRUCTIONS
BODY: Row 1—Ch 17, dc in eighth ch from hook, (ch 2, sk 2 chs, dc in next ch) 3 times. Ch 5, turn.

Rows 2 and 3: (Dc in next dc, ch 2) 3 times, dc in third st of ch. Ch 5, turn.

Row 4: Make 4 sps across as for rows 2 and 3, then work down side of block as follows: 2 sc over side of last dc made, * sc in end of row, ch 7, sk end of next row, sc in end of next row *, 5 sc over corner sp, rep bet *s once more, 2 sc over side of last sp, sl st in corner of block. Turn.

Row 5: (Ch 1, trc in ch-7 sp) 11 times, ch 1, sl st in center of 5 sc, (ch 1, trc in ch-7 sp) 11 times, ch 1, sl st in corner of block.

EDGING: Make 2 sc in sp, ch 3, sl st in top of sc just made for picot, sc in end of row, sc in sp, ch 3 for picot, sc in same sp, sc in end of next row, ch 3 for picot.

Continue in this manner to make picots on alternate sc.

Work around lower part of heart with 2 sc in sps and 1 sc in end of each row, having 5 sc in ch-5 sp at point.

Make 1 sc in each trc and ch-1 sp across the 11 trc at top.

Sk last ch-1 sp before center, ch 25 for hanger, sc in first trc on other side and continue as before. Sl st in first sc and fasten off.

Wax Heart Ornaments

Shown on pages 120 and 121.

MATERIALS
(for 12 ornaments)
½ pound of white tallow wax
White crayon
3½ yards of ¼-inch-wide
   white satin ribbon
12 flat-backed chocolate molds
2-pound coffee can
Large pan to set coffee can in
   (double-boiler-style)
Plastic wrap
Wooden spoon
Measuring cup or small pitcher
Paring knife

INSTRUCTIONS
Caution: Wax is flammable, so keep heat *just above* melting. In case of fire, douse with baking soda.

Note: Use old utensils; wax will be difficult to remove.

Spread newspapers covered with plastic wrap over work surface. Melt wax in coffee can set in large pan filled with simmering water. Add a white crayon to make wax more opaque. Stir when melted with wooden spoon.

For ornament hangers, cut ribbon into 10-inch lengths. Fold each length in half to form loops. Dip 1 inch of cut ends into wax to keep ribbon ends together; set aside to dry. Pour about 1 cup of melted wax into measuring cup or pitcher. Then fill molds to rim. Insert ribbon hangers, holding them several seconds until wax begins to harden.

Allow the ornaments to harden completely before removing them from the molds (about 15 minutes). Pop them out of the molds and trim any rough edges with a paring knife.

Scherenschnitte Ornaments

MATERIALS
Bond or parchment paper
Pencil; cardboard
Utility knife

INSTRUCTIONS
Trace full-size designs, *below,* onto bond or parchment paper with a light pencil. Place the tracing on a cardboard cutting surface and pinprick the dots on the design. Cut small slits for lines with a utility knife. Then, working from the center toward the outside, cut away the blue or outlined shapes inside the design with a knife or cuticle scissors. Finally, cut out the perimeters of the design.

Fabric Heart Ornaments

Shown on pages 120 and 121.

MATERIALS

Old embroidered dish towels and antimacassars or new machine-embroidered fabrics
White fabric (backings)
White lace edging
White thread
Polyester fiberfill

INSTRUCTIONS

Enlarge the heart pattern, *right,* onto paper; cut out.

Cut ornament fronts from worn embroideries that still have pretty sections or cut them from new fabric. Sew white lace edging around hearts ¼ inch from raw edges.

For backs, cut half hearts from white fabric (add ½-inch seam allowances along straight edges). For each back, seam two halves together along the straight edges (center back seam), leaving openings in center of seam. Press the seams open.

With right sides facing, sew the embroidered ornament fronts to plain fabric backs around raw edges (stitch directly over lace stitch line). Clip curves and turn ornaments right side out through openings in center back seams. Press. Stuff hearts with fiberfill and sew closed. Add thread hangers at the ornament tops.

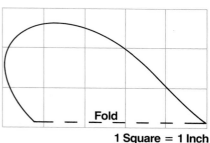

1 Square = 1 Inch

Storing Christmas Ornaments

Keep your holiday tree trims safe by following these storage tips.

Prudent packing
● Stuff padding around ornaments to protect them from damage or breakage. (Wrapping paper scraps work well.) For added protection, wrap ornaments in individual plastic food storage bags.
● Pack decorations in the fold-up storage boxes and chests available at discount stores. Or, ask at grocery stores for case-size boxes (such as those for disposable diapers) and the individual boxes that go inside.
● Lay bows out flat in a box where they won't be crushed. If the bows are slightly wrinkled next year when you unpack them, use a curling iron on a low setting to smooth them out.
● To preserve pinecones, mistletoe, and holly leaves, spray them with clear acrylic.
● Keep hard-to-press stockings from becoming wrinkled by stuffing them with tissue paper or old pantyhose. Cover them with plastic and hang them in the attic. Cover wreaths and hang them up, too.

Safe storage
● Be sure your attic is well ventilated before you store candles or other heat-sensitive items there.
  If you plan to store boxes of trims in the basement, set the boxes up off the floor to cut down on problems with bugs and moisture.
● Once everything is packed, label each box, then jot down the total number of boxes so you'll know how many to look for next year.

Plaid Heart Ornaments

MATERIALS
(for 24 hearts)
¼ yard each of plaid fabric
   and muslin
Polyester fiberfill
6 yards of ⅛-inch-wide
   satin ribbon

INSTRUCTIONS
Use either the small full-size heart shape or the medium full-size heart shape, both on page 128, for the ornaments. Trace the heart shape onto the wrong side of the fabric, repeating for each of 24 ornaments. Do not cut out. Place the muslin to the right side of the plaid fabric. Machine-stitch around the entire heart outline.

Cut out shapes, ¼ inch from the seam allowances. Clip the curves. Make a small slit in the center of the muslin; turn the heart right side out. Stuff the ornament lightly; hand-stitch the opening closed.

Thread a tapestry needle with a 10-inch piece of the ribbon; slip through the center top of the heart. Knot the ends of the ribbon to form a loop for hanging.

Scherenschnitte Dove Ornaments

Dove ornaments measure 3½x4 inches.

MATERIALS
4x5-inch piece of parchment
   paper
Gold embroidery thread
Tracing paper; carbon paper
Small, pointed scissors
Mat knife; stapler

INSTRUCTIONS
Trace full-size pattern for dove on page 128 onto tracing paper.

Using carbon paper, transfer design to parchment paper. *Note:* Cut two identical designs at one time by stapling two pieces of parchment together.

Using a mat knife, cut out all inside markings. Cut around the outside lines using small scissors. *Note:* Cut to the inside of all lines so that no transfer lines show on the finished pieces.

Hang doves with gold thread or frame.

Cinnamon Ornaments

MATERIALS
(for 5 to 8 ornaments)
½ cup applesauce
9 teaspoons to ½ cup cinnamon
   and nutmeg (nutmeg is
   optional)
Cookie cutters
Emboss Art paints and
   decorating tool

INSTRUCTIONS
Squeeze applesauce through the muslin. Mix 1 teaspoon of cinnamon at a time into the applesauce until the mixtureis stiff.

Roll the mixture between two pieces of waxed paper until it is ¼ inch thick. Cut out shapes using cookie cutters.

Bake the cinnamon shapes at 250° for 2 to 4 hours. Turn the ornaments every half hour.

Decorate the cooled ornaments as desired.

Plaid Heart Ornaments
(Instructions on page 127)

SMALL HEART
for ornaments,

MEDIUM HEART
for heart ornaments

Scherenschnitte Dove Ornaments
(Instructions on page 127)

Wooden Ornaments
(Instructions on page 131)

Center

Center

Center

Wooden Ornaments

Ornaments are 3 to 3½ inches tall.

MATERIALS

Scraps of ¾-inch pine; scrap of 2x2-inch pine (blocks)
Band saw
Acrylic paints in assorted colors
Artist's paintbrushes
Sandpaper; table saw

INSTRUCTIONS

Transfer outlines only of full-size patterns on page 129 to scraps of pine; cut out. Cut fourteen 1⅓-inch square wooden blocks from 2x2-inch pine. Sand.

Paint all ornaments with white acrylic to prime. Transfer designs to ornament shapes. Paint motifs, referring to the photograph *opposite* for color suggestions; allow to dry thoroughly. Tape clear nylon thread to back side for hanging.

Embroidered And Crocheted Ornaments

Ornaments are 4 inches in diameter.

MATERIALS

1 inch bone ring (for each ornament)
Knit-Cro-Sheen Cotton thread, Cream and Spanish Red

Size 4 steel crochet hook
14-count ecru Aida cloth
DMC 6-strand embroidery floss
PRYM "Cover Your Own Buttons," Size 60 with rounded edge, 1½ inches in diameter
White Tacky crafts glue
Monofilament

INSTRUCTIONS

FOR EMBROIDERY: Draw 4-inch circles (for each ornament desired) onto ecru Aida fabric. Leave at least 1 inch between circles. Do not cut out. Locate center of circle and center of motif pattern, *right*. Place fabric in hoop and begin stitching at that point. Cross-stitch desired motif, using two strands of embroidery floss over one thread of Aida. Press stitchery; cut out circles.

Cover button following manufacturer's directions.

FOR CROCHET: Rnd 1—Attach cream-colored thread to bone ring; ch 1, work 48 sc in ring; join with sl st to first sc.

Rnd 2: Ch 3, dc in each sc around; join to top of ch-3.

Rnd 3: Ch 3, dc in next 3 dc, ch 5, * dc in next 4 dc, ch 5; rep from * around; join last ch-5 to top of ch-3.

Rnd 4: *Sk next dc, sc in sp bet next 2 dc; in ch-5 lp work 13 dc; rep from * around; join to sc at beg of rnd; fasten off.

Rnd 5: Join red thread in any sc, ch 1, sc in each st around; join to first sc; fasten off. Weave in loose ends.

Arrange outer petals in a clockwise fashion; press.

Glue covered button to center of crocheted portion; allow to dry.

COLOR KEY   **1 Square = 1 Stitch**

⊠ **Green** ⊡ **Yellow**
◌ **Red** ◉ **Brown**

Paper Folk Ornaments

MATERIALS

Assorted plain and printed papers
Gold and white doilies
Red and black fine-point markers
White glue; paper punch
Pencil; scissors; gold thread

INSTRUCTIONS

Using the full-size patterns on page 132, cut dolls and clothing from paper. Glue clothing to bodies. Use a paper punch for the hair and the buttons. Draw on faces with markers.

Paper Folk Ornaments
(Instructions on page 131)

Paper Animal Ornaments

Kids can enliven the family Christmas tree with their very own collection of playful paper critters: puppies, cats, bunnies, and bears.

MATERIALS

Print wallpaper scraps
⅜-inch-diameter shirt buttons
Embroidery floss or other sewing threads that match wallpaper colors
Colored markers
Green carpet thread
Scraps of felt (for bunny and bear scarves)
Scraps of ¼-inch ribbon (for cat bow)
Glue stick
Sewing needle
Scissors
Tracing paper
No. 2 soft-lead pencil

INSTRUCTIONS

Select one of the animal patterns on page 137. Use a pencil to trace onto tracing paper the patterns for the body and the movable arms, legs, or tail. Trace the details of the face and the dots that mark the placement of the buttons. Cut out the patterns.

Cut the wallpaper scraps into 6-inch squares. Using a glue stick, cover the back of one square of wallpaper with glue. Fasten the back of another wallpaper square to the first piece.

If you don't have scraps of wallpaper at your house, visit a wallpaper store and ask about their out-of-date sample books. Most stores give away or charge only a small fee for these books.

Trace the outlines of the animal patterns onto the wallpaper.

Make your own carbon paper on the back of your tracing pattern. (To do this, turn the tissue patterns over and color only on top of the design lines with a No. 2 soft-lead pencil. Do not color the outline shapes.) Use this carbon paper to transfer the face and all other markings to the wallpaper pieces.

With scissors, cut out the wallpaper shapes. Use the needle to punch holes through the dots on the shapes (see photo on page 136, *bottom left*).

Thread the needle with double strands of thread that match the wallpaper. Knot the strands about 2 inches from the end.

Match the dots on *each* body part to the dots on the body. Sew one button to *each* side of the animal to attach the movable parts. Sew through the button, into the arm or leg, through the body, through the arm or leg on the other side, and through another button (see diagram on page 136).

back through the body parts and the two buttons. Knot the ends of the thread. Trim the thread ends to leave 1-inch strands. Repeat this step with the remaining body parts. *Note:* For faster and easier assembly, use ½-inch roundheaded fasteners to attach the arms and legs to the bodies.

With the markers, draw the details of the face on both sides of the animal. Cut a scarf from a wallpaper scrap. Glue the scarf to the dog (see photo on page 136, *bottom right*). Glue a ribbon bow to the cat, and tie felt scarves to the bunny and the bear.

Thread the needle with a 10-inch piece of carpet thread. Draw the threaded needle through the dot for the hanger. Remove the needle and knot the ends of the thread together to make a loop for hanging the ornament.

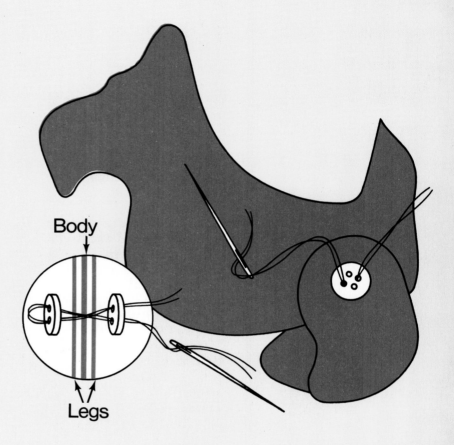

Body

Legs

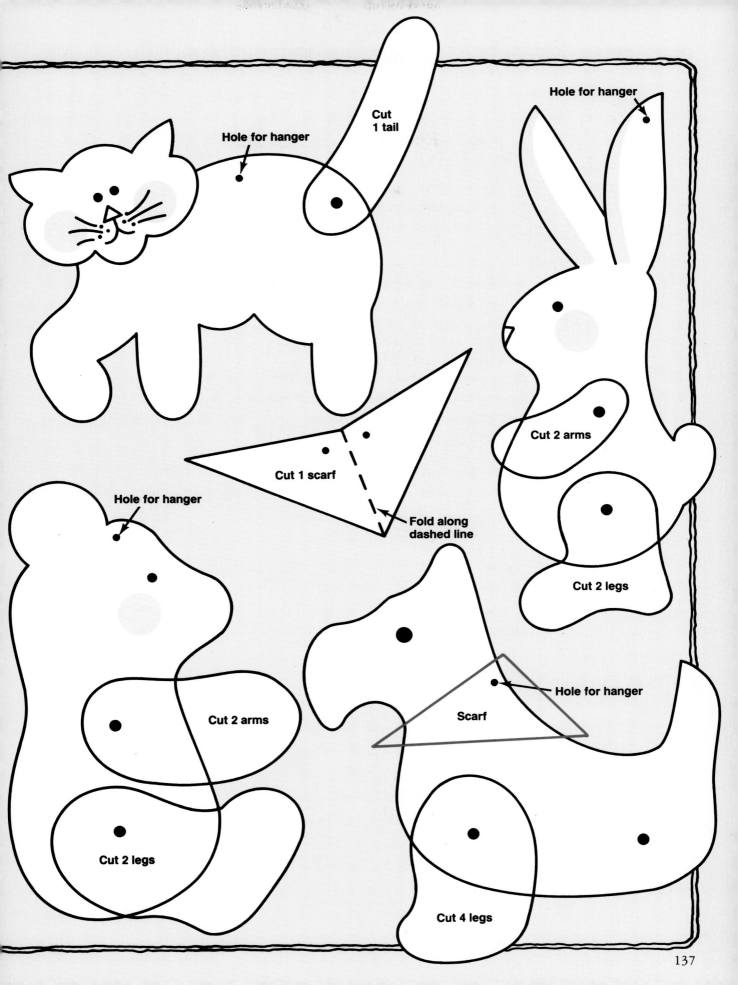

Hole for hanger

Cut 1 tail

Hole for hanger

Cut 2 arms

Cut 1 scarf

Fold along dashed line

Cut 2 legs

Hole for hanger

Cut 2 arms

Scarf

Hole for hanger

Cut 2 legs

Cut 4 legs

The New Nutcracker Suite

A little girl marched around her Christmas tree,
And many a marvelous toy had she.
There were cornucopias of sugarplums,
And a mouse with a crown, that sucked its thumbs,
And a fascinating Russian folderol,
Which was a doll inside a doll inside a doll inside a doll,
And a posy as gay as the Christmas lights,
And a picture book of the Arabian nights,
And a painted, silken Chinese fan—
But the one she loved was the nutcracker man.
She thought about him when she went to bed,
With his great long legs and his funny little head,
So she crept downstairs for a last good night,
And arrived in the middle of a furious fight.
The royal mouse that sucked its thumbs
Led an army of mice with swords and drums.

They were battling to seize the toys as slaves
To wait upon them in their secret caves.
The nutcracker man cracked many a crown,
But they overwhelmed him, they whelmed him down,
They were cramming him into a hole in the floor
When the little girl tiptoed to the door.
She had one talent that made her proud,
She could miaow like a cat, and now she miaowed.
A miaow so fierce, a miaow so feline,
That the mice fled home in squealing beeline.
The nutcracker man cracked a hickory nut
To see if his jaws would open and shut,
Then he cracked another and he didn't wince,
And he turned like that! into a handsome prince,
And the toys came dancing from the Christmas tree
To celebrate the famous victory.

—*Ogden Nash*

CHRISTMAS GAZETTE

Keeping Christmas:
TRADITIONS

Traditions, whether passed along from generation to generation or newly initiated, make wonderful Christmas memories. Draw on your family's heritage, the hobbies and interests of family members, or the desire for shared activities to create holiday traditions of your own. See the next four pages for ideas.

Good Neighbors
Organize the neighbors on your block to line the sides of the street with luminarias on Christmas Eve. Everyone helps pay for the bags, the sand, and the candles, and pitches in extra for a charity.

City Lights
Since 1949, Seattle's Civic Christmas Ship, aglow with holiday lights and a tree, has cruised the city's waterways for several special days in December. The ship, with its passenger load of carolers, makes as many as 25 stops to serenade neighbor-

hoods along the city's glorious waterfront.

A brilliant show of lights ushers in the season in Fort Worth, Texas, as hundreds of cars, horse-drawn carriages, and floats are draped in colored lights and parade up

historical Main Street. The highlight of the celebration is the lighting of the city's Christmas tree.

Every Christmas Eve in Tularosa, New Mexico, luminarias are made and placed the length of the highway that goes through town. Motorists are asked to dim their lights as they drive through to view the beautiful sight.

A special-for-kids parade kicks off the holiday season in Dayton, Ohio. On the Sunday that follows Thanksgiving, downtown streets fill with clowns, marching bands, and floats to the delight of more than 150,000 spectators. A float carrying Santa Claus into the city crowns the day.

Special Celebrations
Step back in time at Colonial Williamsburg (Williamsburg, Virginia), where holiday festivities include costumed entertainers and conjurers, decorated buildings open for tour, and caroling by bonfire light.
Visit the Henry Ford Museum and Greenfield Village in Dearborn, Michigan, which

salutes the season with special exhibits and sleigh rides through the quaint village.
At Mystic Seaport, in Connecticut, costumed guides lead tours at the maritime museum. Tours for kids include chestnut roasting.
Celebrate Christmas on board ship. Cruise

the Mississippi aboard the *Delta Queen* or *Mississippi Queen.* Or, plan a holiday cruise to tropical ports aboard a cruise line with holiday sailings planned.
Parades, decorations, and special shows are among the gala festivities you'll find at

California's Disneyland and Florida's Disney World each Christmas.

Tree Trimming
Label all of your Christmas ornaments with the date and origin to make tree trimming a trip down memory lane.
World travelers: trim a tree with small flags from foreign countries you've visited.
Each Christmas allow your children to select an ornament from the family tree to keep before taking down the tree. When the kids are grown, they will have their own collection of trims and a childhood reminder.
Buy a small living tree. After the holidays, plant it in your yard. Your best bet will be a tree no larger than 2 feet tall. Select yours at a garden center, a

Christmas tree lot, or by mail. Make sure the variety of tree you buy will grow in your area.
A tree for the birds: Bedeck a tree with popcorn balls, pinecones coated with

peanut butter and birdseed, and ropes of raisins, each tied with red yarn.

World View
During the week after Christmas, thousands of families celebrate Kwanzaa, a 20-year-old, non-religious African-American tradition focusing on the family.

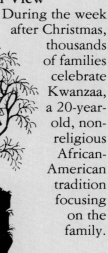

Each day, a candle is lighted to honor one of seven guiding principles, such as unity, creativity, and faith. A feast caps the week.

Choose a foreign country to cele- brate each Christmas. Adopt the country's holiday customs, foods, costumes, history, and traditions for the holiday season.

Borrow a European custom and decorate a tree for the birds this Christmas. Trim an evergreen with edible ornaments, such as orange slices, alphabet breadsticks, bread cookies spread with peanut butter, and cranberry, carrot, and popcorn garlands.

Food Fair

Bake a birthday cake to serve at your family's Christmas Eve meal, in honor of the birth of Christ.

Lay out exotic nibbles—hot spiced sardines, oysters, smoked clams—for

Santa instead of cookies and milk.

Bake cookies for Grandmother to thank her for all the years *she* did

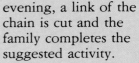

the baking for every- one else.

Invite a group of friends to prepare and sample a traditional recipe that reflects your family's heritage.

Set an extra place at the Christmas table, symbolizing willingness to take in strangers seeking shelter.

Follow the tradition of a Greek family, whose grandmother inserts a coin wrapped

in foil or plastic in a special sweet bread. The coin is supposed to bring good luck for the coming

year to the person who receives it.

Family Festivities

Cut colorful strips of construction paper for each of the 25 days until Christmas and write simple family activities on each. Then, join the strips to create a gaily colored chain that hangs over the mantel. Each

evening, a link of the chain is cut and the family completes the suggested activity.

Make your own Christmas gift wraps and cards. Using a roll of plain butcher paper, tempera paint, and a couple of sponges cut into Christmas shapes, dip one side in paint and stamp away.

For shared good times youngsters will love, why not revive the art of telling tales. Dust off a copy of Dickens' *A Christmas Carol* and read one chapter each evening. Or, share a favorite story from seasons past. You might also take a trip to the bookstore so the children can start on their own memories.

Some new classics to consider: *A Child's Christmas Treasury* (Dial Books), a collection of poems, paintings, and stories that capture the best of holidays past and present; "Good King Wenceslas," the vintage Christmas carol, comes to life in this picture book (E.P.

Dutton Publishers) for young children; and *The Santa Clauses* (Dial Books), a lively new answer to the age-old question: Is there really a Santa Claus?

For a seasonal treat that's as warm and cozy as snuggling up in front of a fireplace, gather the family around the TV to view a classic holiday film. Available on videocassette, these get good ratings: *It's a Wonderful Life, Miracle on 34th Street, A Christmas Carol,* and *White Christmas.*

Holiday Goodwill

Adopt a needy family. Check with local social service agencies for information.

Sing Christmas carols and distribute homemade cookies at a local nursing home.

Participate in Project Angel Tree, which spreads holiday cheer to a special group of children: sons and daughters of prison inmates. Local groups set up trees trimmed with paper angels that hold the names and wishes of children in the area. Then community members file by to pluck an ornament—and make that child's wish come true. To find a project in your area, write:

Project Angel Tree, P.O. Box 17500, Washington, DC 20041.

Each year, countless kids lick envelopes addressed to Santa Claus and send off their sealed wishes. So, where do those wish lists land? Many of them are scooped up by Santa's unheralded helpers at U.S. post offices acros the country. Volunteers sort through the letters, looking for those that demonstrate a need (and have a return address). The letters then are made available to anyone who wants to provide an item on the list—or simply make the holidays brighter in any way they can. Call your local post office for details.

Seasonal Gatherings

Invite neighbors for an evening of carol singing followed by a festive potluck.

Gather family and friends for a holiday reading of Charles Dickens' *A Christmas Carol,* with guests taking roles in the production.

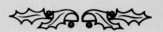

Nativity Scene

Plan and take part in a living nativity for your church during the Christmas holidays.

Greeting Cards

Establish a holiday tradition by making your own Christmas cards each year. One idea: Using paper, tempera paint, and a couple of sponges cut into Christmas shapes, dip one side in paint and stamp away.

Cookies by The Dozens

It's a yuletide tradition in many families: a day or two set aside each year before the holiday hubbub begins solely for the pleasure of baking—and nibbling—batches of their favorite Christmas cookies. It's a tradition worth sharing with friends, as well. On the following pages, you'll find a collection of cookies so irresistible they're certain to become new family favorites.

Pictured at left in assorted shapes and sizes are *German Anise Cookies.*

145

German Anise Cookies

Set aside a day or two before Christmas as "cookie day" at your house, then invite the whole family over to bake and decorate their favorite cookies.

4 cups all-purpose flour
1 tablespoon baking powder
½ teaspoon salt
¾ cup butter *or* margarine
⅔ cup shortening
1½ cups sugar
2 eggs
2 tablespoons milk
2 teaspoons vanilla
8 to 12 drops anise oil
  Boiled frosting
  Decorative candy and
    sugars

Stir together flour, baking powder, and salt. In a large mixer bowl beat butter and shortening till butter is softened. Add sugar and beat till fluffy. Add eggs, milk, vanilla, and anise oil; beat well. Add flour mixture and beat till well mixed. Divide dough in half. Cover and chill for at least 3 hours or till easy to handle. On a floured surface roll dough ⅛ inch thick. Cut with cookie cutters. Place on an ungreased cookie sheet. Bake in a 375° oven for 7 to 8 minutes or till done. Remove from oven and cool. Spread with Boiled Frosting; decorate as desired. Makes 6 to 8 dozen.

Boiled Frosting: In a medium saucepan cook 2 cups *sugar,* ¾ cup *water,* 1 tablespoon *corn syrup,* and dash *salt* over low heat, stirring till sugar dissolves. Cover saucepan for 2 to 3 minutes to dissolve sugar crystals on sides of pan. Uncover; clip candy thermometer to side of pan. Continue cooking till mixture reaches 236° (soft-ball stage).

Meanwhile, in a large mixer bowl beat 2 *egg whites* till stiff. Gradually add hot syrup to egg whites, beating constantly. Add 1 teaspoon *vanilla* and continue beating for 2 minutes or till frosting is of spreading consistency. Divide frosting into smaller portions; tint with *food coloring* as desired. Makes about 3½ cups.

Whole Wheat Joe Froggers

Legend has it that Uncle Joe was an old man who made great molasses cookies. The cookies were named Joe Froggers because they were as big and dark as the frogs hopping around Uncle Joe's pond.

2½ cups all-purpose flour
1½ cups whole wheat flour
1½ teaspoons ground ginger
½ teaspoon baking soda
½ teaspoon ground cloves
½ teaspoon ground cinnamon
⅛ teaspoon ground mace
¾ cup butter *or* margarine
1 cup packed brown sugar
¾ cup molasses
¼ cup milk

In a large mixing bowl stir together flours, ginger, baking soda, cloves, cinnamon, and mace. Set mixture aside.

In a large mixer bowl beat butter with an electric mixer on medium speed for 30 seconds. Add brown sugar and beat till fluffy. Stir together molasses and milk. Add flour mixture and molasses mixture alternately to beaten mixture, beating till combined. Cover and chill for several hours or overnight or till easy to handle.

Grease a cookie sheet. Set it aside. On a well-floured surface roll dough ¼ inch thick. Cut with a 4-inch-round cookie cutter. Place 1 inch apart on prepared cookie sheet. Bake in a 350° oven for 10 to 12 minutes or till edges are firm and bottoms are very lightly browned. Cool on cookie sheet for 1 minute. Remove and cool completely on wire racks. Makes about 20.

Chocolate Cutouts

Planning to keep these cookies around for more than a couple of days? You'll find they store better in an airtight container in the freezer.

2 squares (2 ounces) semisweet chocolate
1¾ cups all-purpose flour
1½ teaspoons baking powder
¼ cup shortening
¼ cup butter *or* margarine
¾ cup packed brown sugar
1 egg
1 tablespoon milk
¼ teaspoon coconut flavoring *or* almond extract
Powdered sugar

In a small heavy saucepan melt chocolate over low heat, stirring often. Remove the saucepan from the heat and cool.

In a small bowl stir together flour and baking powder. Set mixture aside.

In a large mixer bowl beat shortening and butter or margarine with an electric mixer on medium speed for 30 seconds. Add brown sugar and beat till fluffy. Add melted chocolate, egg, milk, and coconut flavoring or almond extract and beat well. Gradually add the flour mixture, beating till combined. Divide dough in half. Cover and chill about 3 hours or till easy to handle.

On a lightly floured surface roll dough ⅛ inch thick. Cut into desired shapes with 2-inch cookie cutters. Place 1 inch apart on an ungreased cookie sheet. Bake in a 375° oven for 6 to 8 minutes or till edges are firm and bottoms are very lightly browned. Cool on cookie sheet for 1 minute. Remove and cool completely on wire racks. Sift powdered sugar over cookies. Makes about 60.

Spicy Cream Cheese Cookies

Try mixing a little allspice or nutmeg in with the sugar that's sprinkled over the tops of these soft sugar cookies.

4½ cups all-purpose flour
2 teaspoons baking powder
1 teaspoon baking soda
½ teaspoon ground allspice *or* ground nutmeg
1 cup butter *or* margarine
1 3-ounce package cream cheese, softened
1 cup sugar
1 cup packed brown sugar
2 eggs
1 teaspoon finely shredded lemon peel
1 teaspoon vanilla
¼ cup buttermilk *or* sour milk*
Sugar

In a medium mixing bowl stir together the flour, baking powder, baking soda, and allspice or nutmeg. Set aside.

In a large mixer bowl beat the butter or margarine and cream cheese with an electric mixer on medium speed for 30 seconds. Add the sugar and brown sugar and beat till fluffy. Add the eggs, lemon peel, and vanilla and beat well. Add the flour mixture and buttermilk or sour milk alternately to the beaten mixture, beating till combined. Divide dough in half. Cover and chill about 3 hours or till easy to handle.

On a lightly floured surface roll the dough ⅜ inch thick. Cut with 2- or 3-inch cookie cutters. Place 2½ inches apart on an ungreased cookie sheet. Sprinkle lightly with additional sugar. Bake in a 350° oven for 10 to 12 minutes or till the edges are firm and the bottoms are very lightly browned. Remove and cool completely on wire racks. Makes 54 to 78.

*Note: To make sour milk, combine 1½ teaspoons *lemon juice or vinegar* and enough *milk* to make ½ cup. Let stand for 5 minutes.

Spicy Wheat Wreaths

Pictured opposite.

- 1 cup all-purpose flour
- ¼ teaspoon baking powder
- ½ cup whole wheat flour
- ½ teaspoon ground cinnamon
- ¼ teaspoon ground ginger
  Dash ground cloves
- ¾ cup butter *or* margarine
- ¾ cup sugar
- 1 egg
- 1 teaspoon vanilla
- ½ cup all-purpose flour
- 12 red *or* green candied
  cherries, halved

Combine the 1 cup all-purpose flour and the baking powder. Set mixture aside. Combine the whole wheat flour, cinnamon, ginger, and cloves. Set aside.

In a large mixer bowl beat butter or margarine with an electric mixer on medium speed for 30 seconds. Add sugar and beat till fluffy. Add egg and vanilla; beat well. Gradually add flour-baking powder mixture, beating till combined. Divide dough in half.

Add the whole wheat flour mixture to 1 half, stirring till combined. Add the ½ cup all-purpose flour to the other half, stirring till combined. Cover each half and chill about 30 minutes or till the dough is easy to handle.

On a lightly floured surface roll each half into a 12-inch log. Cut *each* log into *twenty-four* ½-inch pieces. Roll each piece into a 6-inch rope. Place a white rope and a brown rope side by side and twist them together about 6 times. Shape twisted ropes into a circle, gently pinching where ends meet. Place 2 inches apart on an ungreased cookie sheet. Place 1 cherry half over the spot where the ends meet on *each* wreath.

Bake in a 375° oven for 8 to 10 minutes or till the edges are firm and bottoms are lightly browned. Cool on cookie sheet for 1 minute. Remove and cool completely on wire racks. Makes 24.

Refrigerator Cottage Cookies

Cottage cheese is the secret ingredient that makes these cookies doubly moist and cakelike.

- ¾ cup diced mixed candied
  fruits and peels
- ½ cup chopped candied
  pineapple
- ¼ cup brandy
- 1½ cups all-purpose flour
- ½ teaspoon baking powder
- ¼ teaspoon baking soda
- ½ cup butter *or* margarine
- ⅔ cup sugar
- ½ teaspoon vanilla
- 1 egg
- ½ cup cream-style cottage
  cheese
  Walnut *or* pecan halves
  Diced mixed candied fruits
  and peels

In a small bowl combine the ¾ cup candied fruits and peels, candied pineapple, and brandy. Cover; chill overnight.

Meanwhile, in a small mixing bowl combine flour, baking powder, and baking soda. Set aside.

For batter, in a large mixer bowl beat margarine or butter with an electric mixer on medium speed for 30 seconds. Add sugar and vanilla; beat till fluffy. Add egg and cottage cheese; beat till combined. Beat in dry ingredients. Cover; chill overnight.

Stir fruit mixture into the batter. Bake immediately. *Or,* cover and chill batter for up to 3 weeks.

To bake, drop from a level measuring tablespoon onto an ungreased baking sheet. Press a nut half and additional fruits and peels into top of each dough mound. Bake cookies in a 375° oven for 9 to 11 minutes or till the bottoms are lightly browned and the tops spring back when lightly touched. Serve the cookies warm.

Or, cool completely on a wire rack. Place in a moisture- and vaporproof freezer container. Seal, label, and freeze cookies for up to 12 months. To serve, let stand, covered, at room temperature till thawed. Makes about 54.

Rolled Sugar Cookies

Pictured opposite, clockwise from top left, are Chocolate Sugar Cookies, Cherry-Cheese Rounds, Cookies on a String, and Caramel Nut Sticks.

    2 cups all-purpose flour
1½ teaspoons baking powder
    ¼ teaspoon salt
    6 tablespoons margarine *or* butter
    ⅓ cup shortening
    ¾ cup sugar
    1 egg
    1 tablespoon milk
    1 teaspoon vanilla

Combine the flour, baking powder, and salt. Beat the margarine and shortening till margarine is softened. Add the sugar and beat till fluffy. Add the egg, milk, and vanilla; beat well. Add the flour mixture; beat till well mixed. Divide the dough in half. Cover; chill for at least 3 hours or till easy to handle. Roll the dough ⅛ inch thick. Cut with floured cookie cutters. Place on an ungreased cookie sheet. Bake in a 375° oven for 7 to 8 minutes. Cool on a wire rack. Decorate the cookies as desired. Makes 36 to 48.

Caramel Nut Sticks: Prepare the dough as directed. Roll out half the dough into a 12x11-inch rectangle. Cut the dough into 2x1-inch strips with a fluted pastry wheel. Place the dough on an ungreased cookie sheet; bake as directed above. Roll out remaining dough as before, cut into strips, and sprinkle ¼ cup *finely chopped pecans* over top; bake as before.

For filling, in a small heavy saucepan over low heat, melt 32 *vanilla caramels* with ⅓ cup *milk*. Stir in ¼ cup *finely chopped pecans*. Cool slightly. Spread plain cookies, flat side up, with filling mixture. Top with the remaining cookies, nut side up. Makes 60.

Cookies on a String: Prepare the dough as directed, *except* add 1 to 2 teaspoons *crushed aniseed* to the flour mixture. Roll dough out as directed. Cut out an equal number of 1-inch, 2-inch, and 3-inch star- or petal-shaped cookies. Use a drinking straw to cut a hole in the center of each cookie. Sprinkle the 3-inch cookies with *colored sugar.* Bake all of the cookies as directed. Cool on a rack. Frost 1-inch cookies. When the frosting is dry, string 3 cookies, 1 of each size, on a 6-inch strand of *red shoestring licorice.* Makes 30 stacks.

Cherry-Cheese Rounds: Prepare the dough as directed. Cut out using 2-inch round cookie cutters. Place half of the rounds on an ungreased cookie sheet. For filling, combine ½ of an 8-ounce container *soft-style cream cheese* and 2 tablespoons *chopped maraschino cherries.* Place about 1 teaspoon filling in the center of cookies on a cookie sheet. Top with the remaining cookies. Press cookie edges together using the end of a teaspoon handle. Bake in a 375° oven for 10 minutes. Makes about 28.

Chocolate Sugar Cookies: Prepare the dough as directed, *except* stir in ⅓ cup *unsweetened cocoa powder* with the flour, baking powder, and salt. Roll, cut out, and bake the dough as directed. Makes 36 to 48.

Cookie Frosting: Combine 1 cup sifted *powdered sugar* with enough *milk* (1 to 2 tablespoons) to make frosting of spreading or piping consistency. If desired, stir in a few drops *food coloring.* Makes about ½ cup.

Festive Cookie Dough

Transform this rich, buttery dough into any one or all three of the Christmassy cookies pictured opposite.

3½ cups all-purpose flour
1 teaspoon baking powder
1 cup butter *or* margarine, softened
1 8-ounce package cream cheese, softened
2 cups sugar
1 egg
1 teaspoon vanilla
¼ teaspoon almond extract
¼ teaspoon coconut flavoring (optional)

In a medium mixing bowl stir together flour and baking powder. Set aside.

In a large mixer bowl beat butter or margarine and cream cheese with an electric mixer on medium speed for 30 seconds. Add sugar; beat till fluffy. Add egg, vanilla, almond extract, and coconut flavoring; beat well. Gradually add flour mixture to creamed mixture, beating well after each addition. Divide dough into thirds (about 2 cups each). Cover and chill overnight. Or, place in moisture- and vaporproof plastic bags. Seal, label, and freeze for up to 3 months.

Crackled Crescents

Pictured opposite.

⅓ recipe Festive Cookie Dough
1 6-ounce package (1 cup) miniature semisweet chocolate pieces
1 tablespoon shortening
Chopped coconut, pearl sugar, finely chopped pistachio nuts or finely chopped semisweet chocolate

If frozen, thaw the Festive Cookie Dough in the refrigerator overnight. *Or,* place the dough in a microwave-safe mixing bowl; cover with waxed paper. Micro-cook on 10% power (low) for 5 minutes or till thawed.

If necessary, let dough stand at room temperature for 20 minutes for easier handling. Stir in *½ cup* of the chocolate pieces. Shape dough into 1-inch balls. Roll into logs about 2 inches long. Place logs on an ungreased cookie sheet. Bend and pinch ends to form crescents. Bake in a 375° oven for 8 to 10 minutes or till edges are firm and bottoms are light golden brown. Cool on a wire rack.

In a small heavy saucepan melt the remaining chocolate pieces and shortening over low heat, stirring constantly. Remove from the heat. Dip 1 end of each cookie into the melted chocolate mixture. Roll in coconut, pearl sugar, pistachio nuts, or chopped chocolate. Place the dipped cookies on a cookie sheet lined with waxed paper; chill till the chocolate is set. Makes about 36.

Zigzag Cookie Shapes

If you prefer extra-tender cookies, reroll scraps of dough on a surface dusted with equal parts powdered sugar and flour. Pictured opposite.

⅓ recipe Festive Cookie Dough
1 cup sifted powdered sugar
¼ teaspoon vanilla
Milk
Several drops red food coloring
Several drops green food coloring

If frozen, thaw the Festive Cookie Dough in the refrigerator overnight. *Or,* place the dough in a microwave-safe mixing bowl; cover with waxed paper. Micro-cook on 10% power (low) for 5 minutes or till thawed.

On a lightly floured surface or pastry cloth, roll chilled or thawed dough ⅛ inch thick. Cut with a 2½-inch fluted round or other shaped cookie cutter. Place on an ungreased cookie sheet. Bake in a 375° oven for 6 to 8 minutes or till very light brown around edges. Remove and cool on a wire rack.

To make the glaze to decorate the cookies, in a small mixing bowl stir together the powdered sugar, vanilla, and enough milk (3 to 4 teaspoons) to make a glaze of piping consistency. Divide the glaze in half. To 1 half, add red food coloring; mix well. To other half, add green food coloring; mix well. With a decorating bag and writing tip, pipe both colors over cookies in a random zigzag fashion. Makes about 36.

Little Snow People

No matter the weather—you can build these jolly snow people indoors! They're complete with a dusting of newly fallen "snow." Pictured above.

⅓ **recipe Festive Cookie Dough**
 Miniature semisweet chocolate pieces
 Red cinnamon candies
¾ **cup sifted powdered sugar**
 Milk *or* light cream
 Several drops green food coloring
 Milk chocolate kisses *or* bite-size chocolate-covered peanut butter cups, halved
 Sifted powdered sugar

If frozen, thaw the Festive Cookie Dough in the refrigerator overnight. *Or,* place the dough in a microwave-safe mixing bowl; cover with waxed paper. Micro-cook on 10% power (low) for 5 minutes or till thawed.

For each snow person, shape dough into 3 balls: one 1-inch ball, one ¾-inch ball, and one ½-inch ball. Place balls on an ungreased cookie sheet in decreasing sizes with sides touching. Press together slightly. Press 2 chocolate pieces in smallest ball for eyes. Press 1 red cinnamon candy in middle ball and 2 candies in largest ball for buttons. Bake in a 325°

oven about 18 minutes or till edges are firm and bottoms are light golden brown. Cool for 1 minute on baking sheet. Carefully transfer to a wire rack; cool.

To make the icing for decorating the cookies, in a small mixing bowl stir together the ¾ cup powdered sugar and enough milk or light cream (2 to 3 teaspoons) to make an icing of piping consistency. Stir in the green food coloring. To make hats for the snow people, attach halved kisses or peanut butter cups to the heads with icing. With a decorating bag and writing or star tip, pipe bow ties, belts, scarves, or stocking caps on the snow people with the remaining icing. Lightly sprinkle the snow people with powdered sugar. Makes about 16.

Victorian-Style Gingerbread Mansion

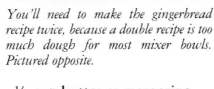

You'll need to make the gingerbread recipe twice, because a double recipe is too much dough for most mixer bowls. Pictured opposite.

½ cup butter *or* margarine
½ cup shortening
1 cup sugar
1 egg
½ cup molasses
2 tablespoons lemon juice
3 cups all-purpose flour
1 cup whole wheat flour
1½ teaspoons ground ginger
1½ teaspoons ground allspice
1 teaspoon baking soda
½ teaspoon salt
Royal Icing

In a large mixer bowl beat butter and shortening with electric mixer on medium speed till softened. Add sugar; beat till fluffy. Add eggs, molasses, and lemon juice; beat well.

Combine the flours, ginger, allspice, baking soda, and salt. Gradually add to butter mixture; beat well. Divide dough in half; wrap in clear plastic wrap. Chill for 3 hours or till firm enough to roll out. Repeat recipe; chill dough.

To assemble the house, construct the individual sections first. Then, join all of the pieces for the bay window, the side porch, and the main portion of the house separately, letting the frosting dry completely before joining these three sections together. Using a star tip in a pastry bag, pipe icing on each edge that will join with another piece as shown below.

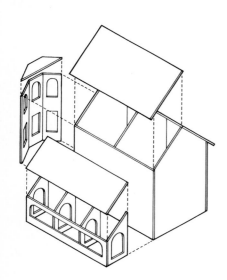

Meanwhile, enlarge the pattern pieces as described on page 156. Turn the oven to 375°. Grease the *outside* bottom of a 15½x10½x2-inch baking pan. Roll out ¼ of the dough on the back of the prepared pan. Place the patterns on the dough. Cut around the patterns with a sharp knife, removing the excess dough from the baking pan. Bake in the 375° oven for 10 to 12 minutes. Let cool on baking pans for 1 minute. Transfer to a wire rack. Repeat with remaining dough and patterns till all of the house pieces are baked.

To assemble the house, decorate each piece with icing, as shown on page 157, using a pastry tube fitted with a round tip. To join pieces together, pipe icing on outside edges of pieces as shown on page 157, using a pastry tube fitted with a star tip. Pipe icing on edges of roof and joining corners of house, using a pastry tube fitted with a star tip. Makes 1 house.

Royal Icing

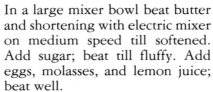

3 egg whites
1 16-ounce package powdered sugar, sifted
1 teaspoon vanilla
½ teaspoon cream of tartar

In a large mixer bowl combine egg whites, sugar, vanilla, and cream of tartar. Beat with an electric mixer on high speed for 7 to 10 minutes or till very stiff. Use at once. Cover icing in bowl at all times with wet paper towels to prevent drying. Makes 4 cups.

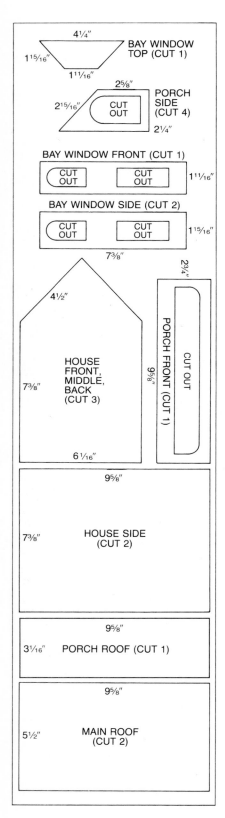

BAY WINDOW
TOP (CUT 1)
4¼"
1¹⁵⁄₁₆"
1¹¹⁄₁₆"

PORCH
SIDE
(CUT 4)
2⁵⁄₈"
2¹⁵⁄₁₆"
CUT
OUT
2¼"

BAY WINDOW FRONT (CUT 1)
CUT
OUT
CUT
OUT
1¹¹⁄₁₆"

BAY WINDOW SIDE (CUT 2)
CUT
OUT
CUT
OUT
1¹⁵⁄₁₆"
7³⁄₈"

HOUSE
FRONT,
MIDDLE,
BACK
(CUT 3)
4½"
7³⁄₈"
6¹⁄₁₆"

PORCH FRONT (CUT 1)
CUT OUT
2¾"
9⁵⁄₈"

HOUSE SIDE
(CUT 2)
9⁵⁄₈"
7³⁄₈"

PORCH ROOF (CUT 1)
9⁵⁄₈"
3¹⁄₁₆"

MAIN ROOF
(CUT 2)
9⁵⁄₈"
5½"

Be sure to cool the gingerbread completely before assembling the house. If you allow the pieces to dry overnight, they will be firm for construction.

Icing

Prepare the Royal Icing (see recipe, page 155). Place a round tip in a pastry bag. Fill the bag with icing. Pipe lines and dots on each piece of the house, using the diagrams shown *opposite* as guides. Be sure the smooth side of the gingerbread is facing you.

Assembly

To assemble the house, first construct the individual sections. Then, join all of the pieces for the bay window, side porch, and main portion of the house separately, letting the frosting dry completely before joining the three sections together. Using a star tip in a pastry bag, pipe icing on each edge that will join with another piece, as shown *opposite.*

Secure the pieces that are being joined together by supporting them at the outer edges with bits of children's nontoxic clay. Keep the supports in place until the frosting has dried and the pieces are secure. (Note: Be sure to keep the unused frosting covered.)

Finishing Touches

Pipe a border around the edges of the roof and the corners of the house and porch. Place the house on some foil-covered cardboard. If desired, pipe some frosting onto waxed paper to resemble a rail fence; stud with chopped nuts. When the fence is dry, remove it from the paper and place it around the house; support with clay.

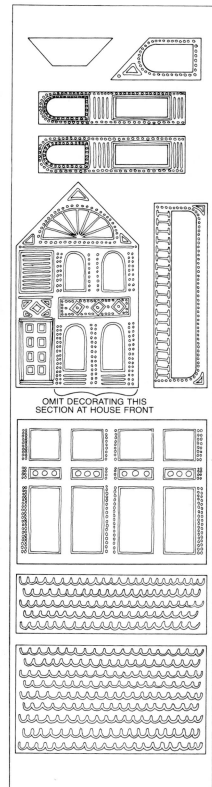

OMIT DECORATING THIS
SECTION AT HOUSE FRONT

The Christmas Puppy

—Kathryn Jackson

Once there was a puppy who lived in an alley between two brick walls. He ate whatever he found to eat, and he slept in a small empty box.

"It's quite a good bed," said the little puppy.

But one morning he woke up shivering. It was cold in the empty box. The north wind blew through the cracks and cried, "Get up, little puppy! It's winter now and you'll have to find a warmer home."

"That's just what I'll do," barked the little puppy, as he tumbled out of the empty box. "This is the day before Christmas. I'll find a nice warm home for my Christmas present."

He ran out of the alley looking for a warm new home.

When he saw some boys throwing snowballs, he ran right up to them. "Who wants a puppy for Christmas?" he barked.

But the boys only laughed and threw more snowballs. One snowball knocked the little puppy over and over in the snow. He scrambled to his feet.

"I thought boys liked puppies," he thought sadly.

Just then the wind came whistling around the corner. It blew up under the puppy's fur and shook his little ears until they looked like unraveling socks.

"Boys do like puppies," laughed the wind, "but they throw snowballs, too."

The wind twirled the puppy around so he could see a man sitting on a bench. When the puppy ran to him, the man got up and shuffled off through the snow.

And when the puppy tried to follow him, he said, "No, little puppy, you can't go home with me. I have no home either."

"Silly puppy," the wind whispered as it came back with a whooosh!

Now the little puppy ran up to the mailman, who was tramping along with his mail bag full of letters and packages.

"Oh, no, puppy," cried the mailman. "I can't take care of you. I have too many things to take care of already."

The wind blew the puppy out into the slippery street.

"Some people are too busy with packages to bother with little puppies," it whistled, and it tossed the puppy up against a policeman's big foot.

"Here, you," the policeman said. "Get back on the sidewalk before you get hurt."

He put the puppy on a big pile of snow on the sidewalk. There the little puppy felt colder than ever.

It was getting dark, and the lights were coming on in all the stores. People hurried by with their arms full of packages. They laughed in the merriest way, but no one noticed the little puppy.

"Everybody seems too busy to even look at me," he sighed.

And then a little girl ran up to him.

"Oh, Mother," she cried, "look at this darling puppy. Can't I take him home?"

The little puppy's heart leaped for joy.

And then it fell down into his cold little toes, because her mother said:

"A puppy would tear up your dollhouse and scratch the rugs and break all the ornaments on the Christmas tree. Come along!"

The little girl ran back to her mother, and they hurried away in the falling snow.

The wind blew sleet in the puppy's ear.

"Some people have too many things to bother with puppies," sighed the wind as it tumbled him over and over again.

continued

The puppy ran on among hundreds of people and double-hundreds of feet, tramping through the snow. Children scampered from store to store looking at toys in the windows.

"I hope I get that engine," cried a little boy. And a little girl sighed, "I think I will get that beautiful doll!"

"Bow-wow!" barked the little puppy. "Doesn't anybody at all want me for Christmas?"

But only the wind answered him.

"Shush! Some people are too busy wishing to bother with puppies!"

And it pushed him down a side street. The little puppy tried to run into the firehouse, but the wind pushed him back.

"Not there," said the wind. "They have a dog and five little puppies now!"

It blew him past the police station and across the railroad tracks . . . just ahead of a big engine that screamed "Loooooook out! Here I come!"

And then the wind blew the little puppy right out into the country.

It was dark now. The houses were far apart and the snow was deep.

"Oh, dear," he thought, "if I don't find somebody who wants a puppy pretty soon, Christmas will be gone."

"Hurry then," cried the wind, and it blew his woolly ears right out in front of his face.

He ran over a bridge and down a hill. He ran past houses with Christmas trees shining in the windows, with wreaths on the doors and smoking chimneys. Then he saw a dark little house with no Christmas tree in its window, no wreath hung on its door.

"Here, puppy," growled the wind. "If you're bound to be a Christmas present, you should have some Christmas wrappings, too.

It blew a bright piece of red ribbon toward him, and laughed and laughed as it whirled away.

The puppy grabbed the Christmas ribbon and began jumping toward the door of the dark house. The trailing ribbon made two straight tracks from the sidewalk right up to the door.

The puppy barked and barked on the doorstep. But no one opened the door.

"I guess nobody is home," he sighed.

He was too tired to go any farther. So he turned round and round to make a little hollow place for lying down, and then—

A big blanket of snow slid off the roof on top of the little puppy! It covered every bit of him and only the ends of the Christmas ribbon showed where he was.

"I'll freeze to an icicle," thought the little puppy. "I'll never live until I'm somebody's Christmas present! I'll never have a home at all!"

Then he heard voices near the road.

"Oh, Mother," cried a little boy's voice. "Santa Claus came while we were out. See the marks of his sleigh!"

His mother looked down at the ribbon tracks.

"I don't think those are sleigh tracks," she said in a tired way. "I just don't think Santa Claus would come away out here."

But the little boy was sure something magic had happened. He went running up the path.

And then he saw the Christmas ribbon sticking up in the snow. He scooped the puppy out of that snowdrift, red ribbon, cold paws, and all, and held him up for his mother to see.

Then the little boy snuggled that cold little puppy against his woolly jacket.

The tired mother smiled a real smile and ran up the path. Her eyes looked as bright as Christmas tree lights. She put her arms around the little boy and the little puppy.

You did get your present after all," she whispered to her little boy. "Your little Christmas puppy!"

The puppy waggled his icy tail and wiggled his snowy ears and barked.

And the wind laughed merrily.

"Some people are glad to have cold little puppies for Christmas," it said, and away it blew.

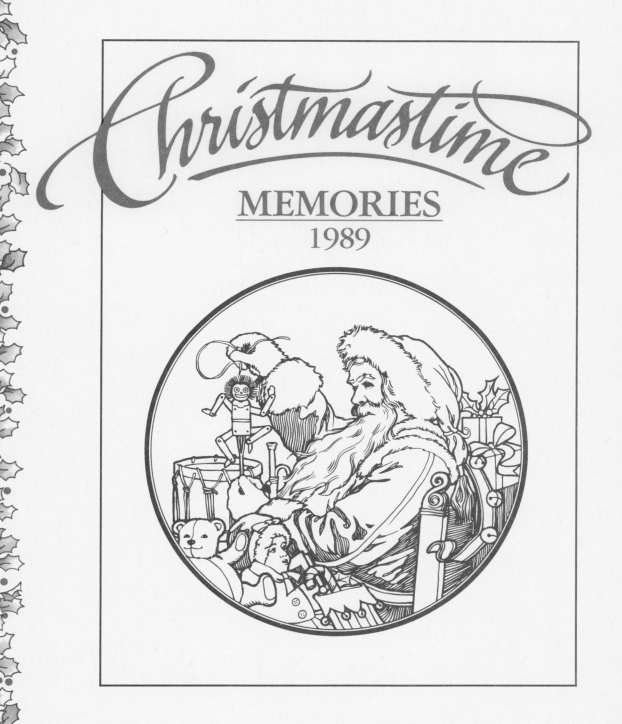

Christmastime

MEMORIES
1989

Christmas Wish List

For family gift ideas

What _____ wants for Christmas _____
_____
_____
_____
_____

What _____ wants for Christmas _____
_____
_____
_____
_____

What _____ wants for Christmas _____
_____
_____
_____
_____

What _____ wants for Christmas _____
_____
_____
_____
_____

What _____ wants for Christmas _____
_____
_____
_____
_____

What _____ wants for Christmas _____

_____

_____

_____

What _____ wants for Christmas _____

_____

_____

_____

_____

What _____ wants for Christmas _____

_____

_____

_____

_____

What _____ wants for Christmas _____

_____

_____

_____

_____

What _____ wants for Christmas _____

_____

_____

_____

_____

Letters to Santa

Dear Santa,

_____
_____
_____
_____
_____
_____
_____
_____
_____
_____
_____
_____
_____
_____
_____
_____
_____
_____
_____
_____
_____
_____
_____
_____
_____
_____
_____
_____
_____
_____
_____
_____

From:

Dear Santa,

_____

_____

_____

_____

_____

_____

_____

_____

_____

_____

_____

_____

_____

_____

_____

_____

_____

_____

_____

_____

_____

_____

From:

Favorite Christmas Memories

Kid's Holiday Artwork

Seasonal Family Activities

Special outings and activities during the holidays

_____
_____
_____
_____
_____
_____
_____
_____
_____
_____
_____
_____
_____
_____
_____
_____
_____
_____
_____
_____
_____
_____
_____
_____
_____

Holiday Get-Togethers

For remembering when we got together with family and friends

Where We Got Together _____

What We Did _____

_____

_____

_____

_____

_____

_____

_____

_____

_____

_____

_____

_____

Where We Got Together _____

What We Did _____

_____

_____

_____

_____

_____

_____

_____

_____

_____

_____

Where We Got Together _____

What We Did _____

_____

_____

_____

_____

_____

_____

_____

_____

_____

_____

_____

Where We Got Together _____

What We Did _____

_____

_____

_____

_____

_____

_____

_____

_____

_____

_____

Holiday Get-Togethers

For remembering when we got together with family and friends

Where We Got Together _____

What We Did _____

_____

_____

_____

_____

_____

_____

_____

_____

_____

_____

_____

Where We Got Together _____

What We Did _____

_____

_____

_____

_____

_____

_____

_____

_____

_____

_____

Christmas Cards

Cards Sent _____

_____

_____

_____

_____

_____

_____

_____

_____

_____

_____

_____

Cards Received _____

_____

_____

_____

_____

_____

_____

_____

_____

_____

_____

_____

Christmas Gifts

Gifts Given

Gifts Received

How We Spent the Holidays

Christmas Eve

Where We Celebrated _____

How We Celebrated _____

_____

_____

_____

_____

_____

_____

_____

_____

_____

_____

_____

_____

_____

_____

_____

_____

_____

_____

_____

_____

_____

Christmas Day

Where We Celebrated _____

How We Celebrated _____

_____

_____

_____

_____

_____

_____

_____

_____

_____

_____

_____

_____

_____

_____

_____

_____

_____

_____

_____

_____

_____

_____

What Christmas Means to Me

_____

_____

_____

_____

_____

_____

_____

_____

_____

_____

_____

_____

_____

_____

_____

_____

_____

_____

_____

_____

_____

_____

Special Moments to Treasure

Photos and other holiday memorabilia

Special Moments to Treasure

Photos and other holiday memorabilia

HOLIDAY DATEBOOK
1989

NOVEMBER

Thursday
23
■ Thanksgiving Day (United States)

Friday
24

Saturday
25

Sunday
26

Monday
27

Tuesday
28

Wednesday
29

Thursday
30

DECEMBER

Friday
1

Saturday
2

Sunday
3

Monday
4

Tuesday
5

Wednesday
6

Thursday
7

Friday
8

Saturday
9

Sunday
10

Monday
11

Tuesday
12

Wednesday
13

Thursday
14

Friday
15

Saturday
16

Sunday
17

Monday
18

Tuesday **19**	
Wednesday **20**	
Thursday **21**	
Friday **22**	
Saturday **23**	
Sunday **24**	■ **Christmas Eve**
Monday **25**	■ **Christmas Day**
Tuesday **26**	■ **Boxing Day (Canada)**
Wednesday **27**	
Thursday **28**	
Friday **29**	
Saturday **30**	
Sunday **31**	
	JANUARY
Monday **1**	■ **New Year's Day**

ACKNOWLEDGMENTS

Editor: Marsha Jahns
Designer: Lynda Haupert
Contributing Writer: Pauline W. Wanderer

We would like to express our gratitude and appreciation to the many people who granted us permission to use their stories, poems, and illustrations in this book.

Pages 10–13: "Christmas Is Coming" by Alison Uttley. Reprinted by permission of Faber and Faber Ltd from THE COUNTRY CHILD by Alison Uttley.

Pages 28–29: Illustration "Falls City Main Street" by John Falter. Reprinted from *The Saturday Evening Post,* Copyright © 1946, The Curtis Publishing Co.

Page 29: "For Christmas" by Rachel Field. Reprinted with permission of Macmillan Publishing Company from POEMS by Rachel Field (New York: Macmillan, 1957).

Pages 34–38: "Ballyutility's Christmas Tree" by Janet McNeill. Reprinted with permission of A.P. Watt Ltd. on behalf of Janet Alexander from A PINCH OF SALT by Janet McNeill.

Pages 62–65: "Carols in Gloustershire" by Laurie Lee. Reprinted by permission of the author and The Hogarth Press from CIDER WITH ROSIE by Laurie Lee.

Page 63: Illustration "Choir Boys" by Francis Tipton Hunter. Reprinted from *The Saturday Evening Post,* Copyright © 1938, The Curtis Publishing Co.

Pages 80–81: "Granny Glittens and Her Amazing Mittens" by Gertrude Crampton from THE TALL BOOK OF CHRISTMAS compiled by Dorothy Hall Smith, Harper and Row, New York, 1954.

Pages 86–87: "A Gift for Gramps" by Aileen Fisher. Reprinted by permission of the author, who controls rights.

Pages 92–95: "The Boy Who Laughed at Santa Claus" by Ogden Nash. From GOOD INTENTIONS by Ogden Nash. Copyright 1937; copyright © renewed 1965 by Ogden Nash. First appeared in *The Ladies' Home Journal.* By permission of Little, Brown and Company.

Pages 114–119: "Christmas Under the Snow" by Olive Thorne Miller. Reprinted courtesy of Houghton Mifflin Company from KRISTY'S QUEER CHRISTMAS by Olive Thorne Miller (Houghton Mifflin, 1904).

Pages 138–139: "The New Nutcracker Suite" by Ogden Nash. Reprinted by permission of Curtis Brown, Ltd. Copyright 1961, 62 by Ogden Nash.

Pages 158–160: "The Christmas Puppy" by Kathryn Jackson from THE ANIMALS' MERRY CHRISTMAS, copyright © 1950, Western Publishing Company, Inc. Used by permission.

Page 159: Illustration "A Boy Meets HIs Dog" by Norman Rockwell. Copyright © Brown & Bigelow USA 1956. All rights reserved.

We would like to extend our sincere thanks to the talented people listed below for their crafts designs and projects:

Page 18: Linda Lindgren (Poinsettia Guest Towels)

Page 19: Dixie Falls (Christmas Greetings Wall Hanging and Greeting Card)

Pages 21–22: Sara Jane Treinen (Star Tree Centerpiece, Star Candlesticks, and Star Centerpiece)

Page 25: Margaret Sindelar (Heart Table Runner)

Page 27: Rebecca Jerdee (Paper-Star-and-Stag Wreath)

Pages 30–33: Ed Wong (Splatter Cards and Christmas Chains)

Pages 66–67: Robyn Knibbe (Animal Sweatshirts)

Page 72: Mary Engelbreit (Embroidered and Appliquéd Stockings)

Page 74: Rebecca Jerdee (Country Doll)

Page 76: Taresia Boernke (Teddy Bear)

Page 78: Dixie Falls (Heart Mittens), Margaret Sindelar (Two-Needle Mittens)

Pages 88–91: Becky Smith (Santa Cookie Puppet)

Pages 120–121: Sandy Moran (Wax Heart Ornaments), Sarah Robinson (Scherenschnitte Ornaments), and Gail Kinkead (Openwork Crocheted Heart Ornaments, Filet-Crocheted Heart Ornaments, and Small Crocheted Heart Ornaments)

Page 126: Margaret Sindelar (Plaid Heart Ornaments), Taresia Boernke (Cinnamon Ornaments), and Kathy Carter (Scherenschnitte Dove Ornaments)

Page 130: Loretta Coverdell (Embroidered and Cross-Stitched Ornaments) and Beverly Rivers (Wooden Ornaments)

Page 133: Bette Welles (Paper Folk Ornaments)

Pages 134–136: Susan Carson (Paper Animal Ornaments)

We also would like to acknowledge the following photographers and illustrators for their creative talents.

Pages 6–7: Perry Struse
Pages 9: John Kelly
Pages 10–11: Photri/Marilyn Gartman Agency, Inc.
Page 35: Helen Kunze
Page 37: Helen Kunze
Pages 58–59: Robert Cushman Hayes
Page 61: Perry Struse
Pages 80–81: Helen Kunze
Pages 92–95: Helen Kunze
Pages 110–111: John Kelly
Pages 116–117: Photri/Marilyn Gartman Agency, Inc.
Pages 138–139: Helen Kunze

INDEX

JUST FOR KIDS

HOLIDAY HINTS AND HISTORY

STORIES

POEMS

MEMORY PAGES

Have BETTER HOMES
AND GARDENS® magazine
delivered to your door.
For information, write to:
MR. ROBERT AUSTIN
P.O. BOX 4536
DES MOINES, IA 50336